3.

Communication in Cancer Care ASH

Communication and Counselling in Health Care

A series of books designed for doctors and allied health professionals. They provide guidance on how to communicate with different patient groups, advice on basic counselling skills, and how to develop rehabilitation programmes.

Other titles in the series:

Communication in Cancer Care

Kathryn Nicholson Perry

Royal North Shore Hospital, Sydney

Mary Burgess

University College London Hospitals NHS Trust

Series Editor: Hilton Davis

BPS Blackwell

© 2002 by Kathryn Nicholson Perry and Mary Burgess
A BPS Blackwell book

350 Main Street, Malden, MA 02148-5018, USA
108 Cowley Road, Oxford OX4 1JF, UK
530 Swanston Street, Carlton South, Victoria 3053, Australia
Kurfürstendamm 57, 10707 Berlin, Germany

First published 2002 by The British Psychological Society and Blackwell
Publishing Ltd

Library of Congress Cataloging-in-Publication Data

Perry, Kathryn Nicholson.
    Communication in cancer care / Kathryn Nicholson Perry, Mary Burgess.
        p. ; cm. — (Communication and counselling in health care)
Includes bibliographical references and index.
    ISBN 1–40510–027–3 (pbk. : alk. paper)
    1. Cancer—Psychological aspects.   2. Medical personnel and patient.
3. Health counseling.
        [DNLM: 1. Neoplasms—psychology.   2. Neoplasms—therapy.   3.
Counseling—methods.   4. Professional–Patient Relations.   QZ 266 P463c
2002]   I. Burgess, Mary.   II. British Psychological Society.   III. Title.
IV. Series.

RC262 .P47 2002
616.99′4′0019—dc21

                                                                2002007793

A catalogue record for this title is available from the British Library.

Set in 10 on 12.5 pt Baskerville
by Ace Filmsetting Ltd, Frome, Somerset
Printed and bound in the United Kingdom
by MPG Books, Bodmin, Cornwall

For further information on
Blackwell Publishing, visit our website:
http://www.blackwellpublishing.com

Dedicated with love to our families: Rollo, Caroline and Fenella (MPJB) and Trevor and Nathan (KNP).

Contents

Preface to the Series

People who suffer serious illness, chronic disease or disability are likely to be confronted by problems that are as much psychological as physical and likely to involve all members of their family as well as their wider social network. They have to adapt psychologically and socially to their circumstances, and this involves significant changes to the ways they perceive themselves and the people around them. This is likely to entail changes to their relationships, lifestyle and aspirations, as well as having to come to terms with an uncertain future. Their adaptation may also influence the effectiveness of the diagnostic and treatment processes and their eventual outcomes.

As a consequence, health care, whether preventive or treatment-orientated, must encompass concern for psychosocial issues, integrated with the physical at all phases of the life cycle and at all stages of disease. The basis of this is an understanding of the processes of supportive communication by all involved in providing services, professionally or voluntarily, underpinned by the skills of empathic listening. These are complex skills and require both training and ongoing supervision for everyone working in health care, from the student to the experienced practitioner.

Although there was a large literature related to counselling and communication when this series of books was initiated in 1991, there were virtually no texts for training purposes related to specific areas of disease. Although the literature has continued to grow within the area of health care, this situation has changed very little. There is still a dearth of material enabling professionals working in specialist areas to explore the processes and skills of communication in ways that practically relate to the problems facing people in their particular field.

The current series was conceived as a practical resource for all who work in health services. The authors of each book have taken a specific area of health care and have provided detailed information from the patient's perspective, about the problems (physical, psychological and social) faced by patients. Each book examines the role of counselling and communication in the process of helping people to come to terms and deal with these problems, and presents usable frameworks as a guide to the helping process. These include detailed and practical descriptions of the major qualities and skills that are required to provide the most effective help for patients and their families.

The intention is to stimulate all potential helpers, whether professional or voluntary, in training or otherwise, to explore and improve their efforts at supportive communication and to find the strength to work in a respectful partnership with the people who need their help. It is hoped that by reading the book, they will become more aware of the patient's situation and the processes of adaptation, and able to contribute positively to their adjustment. The aims of the series will have been achieved if patients and families feel someone has listened, cared for and respected them in their struggle for health. Although physical recovery is of central concern, our purpose includes the effort to make people feel good about themselves, effective, and able to face the future, no matter how bleak, with dignity.

Hilton Davis (February 2002)
Series Editor

Professor of Child Health Psychology at King's College London and the South London and Maudsley NHS Trust and Director of the Centre for Parent and Child Support at Guy's Hospital.

Acknowledgements

Writing a book is a journey in itself, and there are many who have assisted along our path. Thanks are especially due to: the staff and patients of the Cancer Centres at Guy's and St Thomas' Hospital Trust and University College London Hospitals for teaching us so many valuable lessons; Camden and Islington NHS Trust for their support with this project; Professor Hilton Davis for his unstinting encouragement and skilful use of the editor's pen; Professor Michael Richards for his continuing commitment to this important area in the care of people with cancer, and Mr McGregor for offering respite to weary travellers. We should also like to give our grateful thanks to our families for their support and understanding.

Kathryn Nicholson Perry (Sydney, Australia)
and Mary Burgess (London, UK), 2002

The authors and publishers gratefully acknowledge the following for permission to reproduce copyright material:

Extracts from John Diamond (1998), *C Because Cowards Get Cancer Too. . .*, London: Vermilion. Reproduced with permission from Random House.
Figure 3.1 from Michael Parle and Peter Maguire (1995), 'Exploring relationships between cancer, coping and mental health', in *Journal of Psychosocial Oncology*, 13, 27–50. The Haworth Press. Reproduced by permission.

The publishers apologize for any errors or omissions in the above list and would be grateful to be notified of any corrections that should be incorporated in the next edition or reprint of this book.

Foreword

The diagnosis and treatment of cancer can have a devastating impact on the quality of patients' lives and that of their families and carers. Cancer patients face uncertainty and may have to undergo unpleasant and sometimes debilitating treatments. Patients, families and carers need access to support from the time that cancer is first suspected through to death and into bereavement.

In addition to receiving the best available treatments without unnecessary delays, patients give very high priority to other aspects of care. These include being treated with humanity, dignity and respect, being given clear information about their condition and possible treatments, and receiving psychological and practical support when they need it.

Surveys of cancer patients have repeatedly shown that they place particular importance on good face-to-face communication with the health professionals responsible for their care. Research evidence indicates that a willingness to listen and explain is considered by patients to be one of the essential attributes of a health professional, along with sensitivity, approachability, respect and honesty.

As the authors of *Communication in Cancer Care* rightly emphasize, communication is at least as much about listening as speaking. Without good listening skills clinicians may fail to elicit patients' concerns. These concerns may therefore not be addressed and resolved. Similarly if clinicians do not explain effectively why they are suggesting a particular course of treatment, patients may be reluctant to accept the recommendation.

Effective communication is a prerequisite for the delivery of patient-centred care. Increasingly patients want and expect to be partners with health professionals in making decisions about their care. Good communication empowers patients to make informed choices which are right for them as individuals.

Sadly, patients often report poor communication with doctors. If bad news is broken to a patient in an insensitive way this can have a long-lasting negative impact on the relationship between the patient and the doctor. Many complaints by patients and their relatives relate to a perceived failure of health care professionals to communicate adequately or to show they care rather than to problems of clinical competence.

In the past it tended to be assumed that the ability to communicate well was an inborn characteristic. Research has consistently shown that this is not true, but that the necessary skills can be enhanced by training. In recent years schools of medicine and nursing have responded to this by establishing dedicated training programmes within the core curriculum.

Many senior clinicians involved in cancer care recognize that they have received inadequate training in this area. The need for advanced training programmes for senior clinicians was recognised in the NHS Cancer Plan. Work is now underway to ensure that lessons learned from research related to communication skills training are put into practice.

The good news is that the increased emphasis on communication as a key element of cancer care should benefit both patients and health professionals. Consultants who feel inadequately trained in communication skills report high levels of burnout and low levels of job satisfaction.

Communication in Cancer Care will be of interest to a wide range of clinical staff involved in caring for patients with cancer. Written by two health professionals with extensive experience in counselling cancer patients, it sets out the principles underlying effective communication and provides practical advice on how to achieve best practice.

Professor Mike Richards
National Cancer Director

Chapter One

Introduction

Tell anyone that you have cancer and what they'll hear is that you're about to die.
Why would they not? It's what you heard when you got the diagnosis, after all.

John Diamond, 1998

What is the Book about?

This book concerns itself with the impact of cancer on patients and the role of health professionals in relation to it. People with cancer experience a wide range of difficulties and problems associated with their disease. These include problems with everyday practical issues, such as managing to continue running their home or look after themselves. They also commonly feel uninformed about their situation, lacking the information they need to make sense of their situation or to make basic decisions about how to manage day-to-day activities. Finally, they experience high levels of psychological distress and psychiatric morbidity.

These might be considered as the unmet needs of the person with cancer – help with practical problems, information and emotional support. Health services generally concentrate, rightly, on the investigation and treatment of health problems. However, the additional problems experienced by patients can have a significant impact on these activities. They can result in poorer health outcomes, with compromised recovery from treatments, reduced likelihood of adherence to treatment plans and possibly poorer long-term survival. They can impair a patient's ability to function in various roles in the home, at work and in relationships with others. Finally, they can lead patients to be less satisfied with their care and to complain about it. We hope that the book will help health professionals to better understand both their patients' situations and what they themselves can do to avoid or alleviate some of the common difficulties associated with having cancer.

As well as helping to improve the situation for patients, we would also hope that the book will directly assist health professionals in dealing confidently with the situations that they find the most difficult. These include managing uncertainty, breaking bad news, dealing with distressed patients or those with significant psychological problems, and conflicts with other members of the health care team (Faulkner and Maguire 1994). Medical staff have been seen to distance themselves from their patients with cancer. This may be in a bid to protect themselves from the emotional costs of this type of work (Maguire 1989) or because of a sense of not being competent to manage the emotional reactions of their patients. Having a better understanding of patients' situations, a broader range of skills and the confidence to use them can help to alleviate some of the health professionals' own anxieties about discussing sensitive issues.

Distress in Patients with Cancer – an Unmet Need

A large number of studies have been undertaken to try to find out whether people with cancer experience psychological distress as a result. It can be difficult to interpret the findings because of the different ways of measuring distress that have been used and the different criteria for counting someone as distressed. There is also an overlap between the symptoms of psychological distress and those of cancer (for example fatigue, appetite loss and lethargy), and this can result in errors in categorizing patients as distressed.

In spite of these methodological difficulties with the research, it is firmly established that compared to the general population, people diagnosed and treated for cancer have an increased risk of developing anxiety and depression. Approximately 25 to 40 per cent of people living with cancer experience mood changes which are significant enough to warrant formal treatments (Ramirez et al. 1995), be they talking therapies or tablets. Such changes are often called adjustment disorders, which are most common in the weeks following diagnosis, and account for most of the distress identified in people with cancer. Emotional responses exist on a continuum; for example, everyone experiences 'the blues', those brief periods of feeling down, and some will be unlucky enough to experience the severest of depressions, when basic everyday activities of life seem too much and life has lost all its pleasure.

John Diamond (1998) described the depression he experienced:

> I would lie in bed calculating how best to do away with myself. I knew, for instance, that I had a bottle of sleeping pills somewhere which I could crush up and pump into my stomach: one afternoon I went as far as to count them and look up lethal dosages in one of my medical books. It seemed, in those days, such a reasonable thing to do – to let it all just slip away from me.

These emotional difficulties can sometimes be dismissed as rational or normal because they are common. Equally health professionals may not believe themselves competent to deal with emotionally charged situations. As a result, health professionals may not attend to the symptoms of depression that a patient experiences, identify those who are suffering or offer the range of effective interventions from which they might benefit. However, rather than focusing solely on identifying patients with significant psychiatric disorders for specialist interventions, we are advocating the routine use of communication and counselling skills for the benefit of all.

Why are there Unmet Needs?

In part it is because these aspects of the patient's experience are not routinely on the health care agenda. Patients and health professionals do not discuss these unmet needs. In part, health professionals do not raise emotional, information and practical needs with patients. Equally, patients may be disinclined to tell the health professionals about their psychosocial or practical problems.

There are a number of possible reasons why professionals do not discuss these matters with their patients. It may be partly to do with the expectation that all patients feel low or anxious, and so there is no need to ask about it. Linked to this are the beliefs that as a rational response to an unpleasant event, such mood changes do not warrant intervention or would not respond to any interventions offered. In addition, health professionals often think, with some cause given the amount of routine training they have in communication skills, that they do not have the necessary skills or confidence to discuss sensitive issues with their patients, and hesitate to do so.

Patients' reluctance to talk to their health professionals about these matters may, in part, be because of fear: fear that they are going mad or that they are inadequate, and that their treatment may be stopped if they are 'not coping' with it. The relationship between patients and their health professionals will also make a difference to whether they feel able to raise sensitive issues.

In addition, a number of other service issues contribute to these needs not being identified and met. These include poor continuity of care, with a large number of staff involved in the care of the patient. This can make it difficult for the patient to get to know anyone sufficiently to discuss sensitive issues, and sub-optimal communication between health professionals can mean that some of these issues are not followed up. There is also time pressure in the health service because of the inadequate supply of suitably qualified staff in many areas.

How can we Help Patients Address these Needs?

There are a range of strategies that can be used to better meet patients' needs. There has been a trend to try to include mental health and counselling staff in oncology clinics as a form of adjuvant treatment. However, while this is clearly necessary for some patients with significant levels of distress, it can have the effect of splitting off emotional issues from the rest of the patient's care. A more integrated approach is favoured, ensuring that routine healthcare practice includes effective communication about the disease, its impact and the help that is available, with referral made to specialists if necessary. Specifically, this includes the provision of adequate information and help in obtaining the practical assistance needed to cope. It also involves routinely asking about patients' emotional reactions to their disease and its management. This in itself can help to create the sort of relationship between a health professional and a patient which enables the patient to raise such concerns. This opens the door for the health professional to assist the patient in dealing with these concerns. Health professionals can improve their ability to identify those patients experiencing significant psychological difficulties, and speedily refer them for assessment and intervention.

Such strategies have communication as their base. They are dependent upon the health professional's ability to engage the patient and enable free and open discussion. It is important, therefore, that all professionals are selected for, trained and supported in using counselling and communication skills.

What are Counselling and Communication Skills?

Egan (1998) describes the process of counselling as having two main goals:

1   to help clients manage their problems in living more effectively and develop unused or underused opportunities more fully; and
2   to help clients become better at helping themselves in their everyday lives.

The words counselling and communication are used in a wide range of situations to mean any number of related activities. Large numbers of people seek help from a professional counsellor to help them deal with 'developmental issues, addressing and resolving specific problems, making decisions, coping with crisis, developing personal insight and knowledge, working through feelings of inner conflict or improving relationships with others' (British Association of Counselling Code of Ethics and Practice for Counsellors). This may be done through regular meetings with the counsellor to explore the reasons for problems and to develop strategies with which to tackle them. This form of ongoing, professional counselling relationship lies at one end of a continuum. At the other end lie the one-off counselling sessions that may be proactively offered in relation to specific events, for example on the risk of developing a genetic disorder or whether to take an HIV test. These are more to do with information provision on a specific topic and the exploration of actions that may be undertaken as a result. However, all are subsumed within the basic goals of Egan's (1998) description.

In the context of this book we are focusing on some of the skills required to address Egan's (1998) goals as they apply to the general helping relationship between professionals and patients with cancer. This includes having the skills to develop an equal relationship with another person based on the idea that patients have the abilities and resources to deal with problems. It involves the systematic use of questions and prompts to help patients tell their story. It crucially consists of the skills of listening carefully, helping patients understand their situation more clearly, and rallying coping resources. These might be called counselling and communication skills, rather than professional counselling, in that they can be used in all interactions by all professionals with all patients.

An example of the use of such skills might be when a patient first visits the general practitioner with a concern about a suspicious symptom. The general practitioner might anticipate the patient's anxiety, and so be careful to orientate the patient by being considerate, courteous and warm. The GP might then ask the patient to explain the reasons for attending, being careful to enquire about whether there are any other concerns. They might then go on to discuss what the patient thought might be needed in terms of investigation and management. They may discuss the possible diagnosis, and whether the explanation was understood by the patient and what it might mean for him or her. Finally, they would agree a plan of action and when it would need to be reviewed.

Managing the consultation in this way the GP is using counselling and communication skills and is likely to be much more effective. This way of working with patients is becoming a general expectation rather than just an ideal held by a few.

The duties of the doctor, as defined by the General Medical Council, include:

- listening to patients and respecting their views;
- giving patients information in a way they can understand;
- respecting the rights of patients to be fully involved in decisions about their care.

Successfully executing each of these duties depends on being able to listen to the patient and elicit their views, as well as express complex ideas about diagnosis and treatment. Therefore the use of communication and counselling skills is something that should be considered in every interaction with patients, not just reserved for those tricky situations with which most health professionals are familiar, such as breaking bad news.

Who is this Book for?

The duty of all doctors, and most other health professionals as set out in their own guidance on standards of practice, includes effective communication as described in the last section. Therefore, learning counselling and communication skills is relevant to all health professionals. The prevalence of cancer is such that there are few health professionals who do not come into contact with patients with the disease. Certainly, general practitioners, practice nurses and health visitors, and nurses, physicians and surgeons in hospitals, are all commonly faced with patients with cancer. There are also those who specialize in cancer care. Any and all of these people may benefit from reviewing and improving their skills. There is certainly evidence that these skills can be learnt, and while a book is not the only way to do it, it can certainly contribute to awareness and act as encouragement to explore other ways in which to access training.

Plan of the Book

The book has three main parts:

1 understanding the role of psychological processes in patients with cancer and their management;
2 understanding the role and process of the helping relationship with patients with cancer; and
3 identifying the skills involved in the helping relationship, and how to apply them.

Finally there is a chapter on some of the issues faced by professionals in cancer care.

We will be using the term 'patient' in this book to describe someone with cancer. This is not because we do not see them as someone with a broader identity, but because we are focusing on people with cancer in medical settings. We will also be using the term 'health professionals' throughout, rather than 'counsellor'. This is to try to avoid any suggestion that this work can only be undertaken by a professional with the title of counsellor. Rather we see these skills as one of the essential tools of any health professional, the use of which will improve the provision of health care in any situation.

We have tried to describe the use of communication and counselling skills when caring for patients with cancer. Perhaps more importantly, we have tried to explain how to develop and use these skills. As with any book concerned with learning skills, reading the book itself is not sufficient. The only way to acquire new skills is to practise using them. Health professionals are not always the best judges of whether they need to improve their communication skills. Your own assessments may not agree with those on the receiving end! Throughout the book we will be providing ideas about how to build up your own skills, and there are suggestions for how to access further training at the end.

You may find it most productive to read through the whole book first. However, we hope that the index will guide you quickly to points of reference when you want to remind yourself of a particular point of practice.

Summary

- Patients with cancer have a significant number of unmet information, practical and emotional needs.
- The consequences of this include poorer health outcomes, reduced well-being and less patient satisfaction with care.
- In addition, although estimates vary, cancer patients experience more psychological distress and psychiatric morbidity than the general population.
- Health professionals often find it difficult to discuss sensitive issues with their patients, and commonly do not feel confident about their use of communication skills.
- Patients are often disinclined to raise issues of concern, including changes in mood, in part because of fears that they are going mad or that it might affect how their cancer is managed.

- The use of general communication and counselling skills in interactions with patients can improve the management of care all round.
- These skills can be used to improve the routine provision of information and practical support to patients.
- Communication and counselling skills can be learnt and used by all healthcare professionals.
- This book aims to describe these skills and explain how to use them in the care of cancer patients.

Chapter Two
Cancer and its Management

The Cancer Journey

From the point at which someone is aware of a symptom which will later be diagnosed as cancer, they are starting their cancer journey. They cannot know at that point how many twists and turns the journey will involve, nor when or how it will finish. However, what is certain is that they will experience changes in both their physical and emotional states. They will have to accustom themselves to medical jargon about their disease. At the start, this will seem impenetrable, and in many cases remains that way. They will be called upon to negotiate the challenges of changes to their roles at home or at work, dependence upon others and, perhaps worst of all, the uncertainty that cancer brings in its wake. Throughout these times of acute vulnerability they will be involved in interactions with health professionals.

This chapter aims to outline some of the key issues in the management of cancer and how they impact upon the emotional lives of the individuals living through them. We will initially review some of the basic facts about cancer, and then trace through the cancer journey from initial symptoms, diagnosis and treatment to what happens when cancer is beyond hope of cure.

What is Cancer?

Although people often have previous experience of cancer, which will help to form their view of their own situation, cancer is a complex disease and misunderstandings are common. Cancer is the name given to a collection of over 200 diseases which share the ability to *metastasize*. Metastasis occurs when cells eventually break away from their original site (known as the *primary*) and travel to other parts of the body where they form secondary cancers. Cancers form when the individual cells fail to die. This means that they reproduce unchecked, causing many more cells to be present than is usual.

They can arise in various tissues in sites throughout the body, and thus they all behave very differently. The word *tumour* is usually used to describe a mass of cells which has formed into a lump. In some cases they are *non-malignant* or *benign* and do not have the ability to metastasize. Those which can metastasize are cancerous, and are referred to as *malignant*. Tumours are also sometimes known as *neoplasms*. Although the complexities in labelling are intended to aid communication between clinicians and researchers, they have also served to create a situation in which people receiving a new diagnosis may naturally become confused about the nature of their condition.

When the process of metastasis occurs, the cancer cells which form secondary cancers in other parts of the body share the same characteristics as the primary cancer. This can be the cause of a common misunderstanding about cancer, as people told of cancer in another area of the body often understand it to mean that they have more than one sort of cancer. They may then compare themselves incorrectly with others who had primary cancers in the site of their own secondaries. Such comparisons can be inaccurate, and either suggest a more favourable or less favourable course than is the case.

Cancer can have diverse effects on both body tissue and the physiological processes carried out by the body. It can destroy tissue or cause blockages, for example in the intestines. It can also disrupt the transmission of oxygen around the body, in the case of leukaemia, or alter metabolic processes carried out by the liver, for example causing hypercalcaemia. The processes of cancers forming and spreading can be associated with different degrees of symptomatology. Awareness of cancer's ability to spread can incline people who have been apparently successfully treated to be very vigilant for changes in their physical state. Every slight pain or change of bowel habit can trigger concerns about its meaning, and they frequently find it hard to reassure themselves or to accept the reassurance of their health care workers.

Different cancers have different *incidence* and *prevalence* rates, but eight million people are living with cancer in the United States of America alone. The incidence of cancer increases with age, with 70 per cent of cancers occurring in people over the age of 60 years. The most common types in developed countries are lung, large bowel, prostate and breast cancers. However, leukaemia is more common in children and testicular cancer more prevalent in young men (CRC 2000).

Different types of cancer are associated with different survival rates, and while some are almost always fatal, in others there is the expectation that the cancer can be at least controlled if not cured. The stage of the cancer, that is the degree to which metastasis has occurred, also provides information about the likely course of the disease. However, each year approximately 50 per cent of cancers are cured (CRC 1996).

Newly diagnosed individuals are often unfamiliar with the specific statistics regarding their disease, and so may draw on inaccurate information to try to make sense of what the cancer means for them. Most of the general population overestimate the likelihood of cancer being fatal. It is therefore no wonder that the immediate aftermath of a diagnosis is the time when distress is likely to be at its highest, but for the majority such distress is transient. For example, in the days following her diagnosis with bowel cancer, Marion, a single mother aged 46 years, felt some of the emotions commonly experienced during this time. She experienced swings in mood, from feeling her normal self to periods of great distress and hopelessness about her future. At times she felt completely cut off from the rest of the world, almost as though she was living within a bubble, and experienced intrusive thoughts of her daughter's distress if she died. She felt less and less confident about managing day-to-day life, and became increasingly unable to take part in life with those around her. These emotional changes made her question her own sanity, and she wondered if she might be going mad. However, six weeks later, following surgery and once adjuvant treatment had begun (treatment intended to supplement the main strategy of removing the tumour itself), Marion's mood swings had settled. Although she continued to worry about the long-term outcome of her cancer, she was able to concentrate on day-to-day life again.

The Path to Diagnosis

There are many different ways in which people find out that they have cancer. They may themselves identify a suspicious symptom and consequently visit their doctor. The following symptoms persisting longer than two weeks may be a cause for concern:

- change in bowel or bladder habits;
- a sore that does not heal;
- unusual bleeding or discharge;
- thickening or lump in the breast or any other part of the body;
- indigestion or difficulty swallowing;
- obvious change in a wart or mole;
- persistent cough or hoarseness.

Identifying symptoms Clearly, all of these symptoms may occur for reasons other than cancer. People often express a strong urge to receive a diagnosis to account for the symptoms they are experiencing and, perhaps most importantly, to suggest treatments to cure the condition diagnosed. The individual's previous experiences and understanding of their symptoms may influence how they interpret and respond to them. Likewise the emotional state of the person can shape their response, and John provides a good illustration of how our beliefs and emotional reactions can shape our experience of physical symptoms.

John was a 48-year-old man who had presented on a number of occasions to a genito-urinary clinic with symptoms which he was concerned were indicative of prostate cancer. His father had had prostate cancer and died recently, aged 84 years. He and his father had discussed the diagnosis only minimally, as John was fearful of hearing anything that might distress him. John had always been alarmed by changes in his body, and attended his general practitioner about minor symptoms regularly. Previously he had always been easily reassured about the benign cause for individual physical changes, but was not convinced that his urinary symptoms were not cancer. He was acutely aware of the need to urinate and monitored it closely. Memories of his father's death intruded into his daily life. His concerns were causing physical symptoms of anxiety, such as racing pulse and hyperventilation, which in turn he had become convinced were signs of serious illness. As he was unable to be so easily reassured on this occasion, he was referred to a mental health professional working within the unit for further assessment.

There are programmes designed to encourage people to monitor themselves for early physical signs of cancer, such as testicular or breast self-examination. Awareness and education about symptoms is often favoured and should be encouraged. However, unlike John, some people may be reluctant to check themselves physically for a number of reasons, including anxiety about finding a symptom and embarrassment. This can result in delayed presentation of symptoms, which may have an impact on the management and outcome of the disease itself.

Elizabeth's mother died at the age of 40 years as a result of breast cancer. Despite thinking that she might be at higher risk for breast cancer because of this, Elizabeth's intense fear of the disease inhibited her from examining herself. She tried hard to avoid thinking about it, but was plagued by memories of her mother's last birthday when she was experiencing a great deal of pain and was very distressed. In the months prior to her own fortieth birthday, Elizabeth became increasingly anxious, but was unable to identify why. It was only during an appointment with her general practitioner for cervical screening, which she attended regularly, that the disparity between her approaches to the two diseases became apparent. As the emotional issues of fear of cancer and the associated memories of her mother's death were her main problems, the GP discussed with her referral to a counsellor to explore the issues further.

There has been a great deal of interest in patients who delay seeking help and advice after becoming aware of a symptom which may be related to cancer. Delaying may be a way to reduce the worry that the symptom signals cancer. There is evidence that in the case of breast cancer, older women are more likely to delay seeking help. Even when symptoms of cancer itself are present and the person visits their doctor promptly, there is evidence that younger women and those with breast symptoms other than a lump may experience delays by service providers (Ramirez et al. 1999).

Screening programmes Increasingly, people are becoming familiar with the idea that detecting cancer in the early stages simplifies management, even if it does not necessarily affect the final outcome of the disease process.

Initiatives such as those for cervical cancer and breast cancer are now widely accepted. Other formal screening programmes are currently being evaluated, such as the use of *flexible sigmoidoscopy* for bowel cancer. They rely on the cancer being common, associated with high-risk groups and having a pre-cancerous condition that is both identifiable and treatable. However, for some rapidly growing cancers, screening can be unsuccessful in detecting a pre-cancerous stage much before symptoms become apparent.

The concepts that underlie screening programmes are complex, and patterns of attendance suggest that they are not fully understood by the target populations. For example, in the case of mammograms as a screening tool for breast cancer, certain social groups are overrepresented in attendance figures with women from middle-class groups being more likely to attend.

As well as social factors, individual factors may be important. Perceptions of personal risk and the degree to which people perceive there to be a solution available can influence individual decisions to attend on the first occasion and for subsequent recalls. There are also the costs of screening programmes to consider. These include the economic costs of providing the service, such as the testing equipment and the administration involved in delivering it. There is some concern that a negative screening result, while not a guarantee that pre-cancerous changes are not taking place, may be seen by some people as such, and thus alter their inclination to seek advice should a suspicious symptom develop.

At times there has been great concern about the emotional effects of screening. Firstly, unnecessary distress may be caused by telling the patient that a cancer might be present when in fact this turns out not to be the case (false positive). Secondly, this may also happen when tests are reported to be clear and the person is later diagnosed with the cancer (false negative). As yet the psychological effects of screening have not been fully documented, but large-scale studies which are currently underway may help to establish the real emotional sequelae of such programmes. In some people even the invitation to take part in a screening programme may cause anxiety, and being alerted to an abnormal result may increase this effect. In general, providing rapid access to health professionals with whom to discuss abnormal results and providing sufficient information for people to make sense of the result are associated with better outcomes in terms of distress levels. There is some evidence that while 'false positives' (being told that a problem has been detected, which is subsequently found not to be the case) cause an increase in distress, once subsequent assessments confirm the result as negative the distress is reduced again (Wardle et al. 1993).

Other forms of screening include testing for genes associated with particular forms of cancer which are genetically transmitted, such as BRCA1 in the case of breast cancer. These technologies are still in the early stages of development, and differ from the others in that they provide information about vulnerability to developing a disease rather than evidence of the presence of disease. Concerns have been raised about the emotional impact of these tests, and this is now commonly being included in the evaluations of the programmes.

Management of Cancer

At some point in the cancer journey, the individual will present to services, perhaps most commonly to the general practitioner in the first instance.

First consultation The initial contact with health professionals concerning a symptom that may indicate cancer is most likely to take place in the general practitioner's surgery. The purpose for both parties is to assess the situation and is likely to result in further investigations and consultations with other health professionals in the hospital setting.

Many people are aware of the idea that humans make quick assessments of new situations, almost without being aware of it. The conclusions we draw in the first few seconds of meeting someone can then colour the future relationship. This highlights the importance of the first time that someone is seen about a suspicious symptom. The emotional distress commonly experienced, whether displayed to the world or masked, can influence the ability to attend to what is happening or being said, make sense of information and weigh up the choices offered. In this emotionally charged atmosphere, issues that may seem small in other situations can take on great significance.

Despite it being fifteen years ago, Rebecca vividly remembered her first appointment at a teaching hospital when she developed symptoms which her general practitioner was concerned might be indicative of bowel cancer. She had been unable to sleep the night before, and her embarrassment about her symptoms had made it impossible for her to share her anxieties with friends who normally provided her with support. On arrival at the hospital, she became lost and so was ten minutes late arriving. Walking into the out-patients department she saw two women sitting in surgical gowns with their clothes by their side. She approached the reception area, and was told that she would have to wait and to take a seat. Two hours later, she too was asked to undress and take her seat again. Some time later she was ushered into a small room, where a group of men in white coats were waiting. One asked her what the problem was and then asked her to lie on a bed to be examined. During the examination he described what he was doing to the others ranged around the bed. Throughout the examination Rebecca felt detached from her body, with the doctors' voices sounding distant from her. He then addressed Rebecca, telling her she would need an operation and she would be sent an appointment in the next week. Although this extreme experience is unlikely to be repeated in the modern health system, Rebecca was plagued by unwanted memories of it for several weeks to come. The intervention was successful in managing her benign condition, but some years later she developed further symptoms. However, these unpleasant memories returned and prevented her from seeking help for nearly six months.

There are clearly a number of basic measures that many departments have now adopted to make the first consultation a less intimidating experience.

These include providing private areas to undress and to be seen in, warning patients about the presence of medical students (and reminding them of their right to be seen without them), the use of name badges and reducing the time that patients have to wait for their appointment.

Diagnostic procedures The vast majority of cases of cancer are diagnosed when the individual seeks help after noticing symptoms. These may be very specific in nature, such as finding a breast lump, or generalized, such as weight loss or lethargy.

It is seldom possible to diagnose cancer on the basis of a single consultation, and individuals are frequently required to attend for a number of investigations. 'One-stop' clinics have recently been set up, for example in breast clinics, to carry out all the required tests on one occasion. In some cases results can be given on the same day. More commonly, people attend a series of appointments. The investigations range from simple tests, such as blood tests or a smear, through the wide variety of scans now available, to invasive procedures, such as biopsies, which may require an in-patient admission. Scans, in particular, can also be used to detect secondary cancers in other sites of the body.

The initial series of investigations is a time when individuals are going through a rapid process of assimilating new information and trying to make sense of the implications for them. In a study of people with inoperable lung cancer, 40 per cent of people were dissatisfied with the level of information they had received (Hughes 1985).

Information about procedures can be provided both about the events which the patient will undergo (procedural information), and also about how the patient will feel as a result of a particular stressful medical procedure (sensory information). Both types of information are important, but generally sensory information seems to be essential (Suls and Wan 1989).

Sarah was 65 years old when she started to develop headaches and difficulties with her vision. Her general practitioner referred her to a neurologist who arranged an MRI scan. Sarah was unfamiliar with the procedure she was to undergo, and became acutely anxious during the scan and found the noises emanating from the machinery particularly distressing. On discussion with the radiographer it became clear that she had long-standing fears of small spaces since several traumatic incidents during wartime use of bomb shelters as a child. The scan had to be abandoned. However, Sarah was able to return on another occasion for a visit to the unit. Following a full explanation and observation of the scanning machine she was able to complete the scan successfully.

The time around diagnosis is also the time when many other general beliefs about cancer rise to the surface, such as that cancer may be contagious or that the sufferer has only themselves to blame for contracting the disease. Such beliefs serve not only to increase the distress of the patient, but also to change both their own and others' behaviours in a way that undermines their adjustment to the news. Believing that others regard you as the cause of your own misfortune, as in the case of a smoker who has developed lung cancer, can reduce attempts to elicit social support at a crucial time.

Treatments Choice of treatment is a complex matter, determined by a multitude of factors, including the type, site and stage of the cancer. A range of specialist medical personnel can be involved in the decision-making process, including *surgeons, medical oncologists, clinical oncologists* and *radiotherapists.* Often a combination of therapies is involved. Treatments such as surgery may aim to eradicate the cancer entirely, and so are known as *radical* treatments. These may be used in conjunction with another treatment, such as chemotherapy, which is then known as an *adjuvant* treatment. There are also treatments used to reduce symptoms, known as *palliative* treatments.

While palliative care and treatment are most commonly used when the cancer is beyond hope of cure, they can also be used to help relieve symptoms earlier in the course of the disease. Anxieties about the implications of particular interventions can be significant for individuals. Bill, who had painful secondaries in his bones, was prescribed morphine-based medication to help manage his pain during a course of chemotherapy which was hoped would put his testicular cancer into remission. However, a few days later his general practitioner was called to his home because of agonizing pain which had distressed both him and his family. On discussion it transpired that Bill had not been taking his medication since a discussion with a friend who told him that a relative had been prescribed morphine shortly before her death from lung cancer. The friend was convinced that the drug had hastened her death, and that it was only used for people who were dying, because of the possibility of addiction. This had alarmed Bill, and so he had resolved not to take it. Consequently his pain problem had escalated, and he had interpreted this to mean that he was likely to die imminently.

The degree of experience of the clinicians has recently been acknowledged as an important predictor of outcome. Therefore, more specialized treatments and rarer cancers are now managed within cancer centres, in which staff are expected to be specifically experienced in the diagnosis and management of cancer. Again, media reports of inadequate services for cancer patients have the potential to create concern in those who fear that their medical team might not be in the best position to treat them effectively.

Samantha, a middle-aged woman with ovarian cancer, attended an appointment for a second opinion arranged by her GP with an oncologist at a teaching hospital. She was accompanied by her husband, Mike, a scientist working for a major drug company. Mike reported that they had also seen a consultant through his company's health care insurance for an opinion about the best way to proceed. He became angry and agitated when the oncologist offered an opinion which differed from the other views they had received.

Decisions about treatment can be very anxiety-provoking, because the perceived risks of making the wrong choice are high. On occasions the anxiety can be expressed as anger at health professionals who are not able to provide the guarantees about successful treatment that the patient craves.

While at times the view has been expressed that different treatments are more or less costly in an emotional sense for the person undergoing them, there is little research evidence to support it. It was hoped, for instance, that the removal of just the tumour and immediate surrounding breast tissue, called a *lumpectomy*, rather than the removal of the whole breast, would result in less distress for women treated for breast cancer. However, that has not proved to be the case (Kiebert et al. 1991). Early in the study of the psychological effects of cancer treatments, the relationship between the degree of distress and particular cancers and treatments was the focus of research. The belief was that most emotional distress would be accounted for by factors specific to the cancer and the treatments received. It has become clear that the relationship is not so straightforward, with other variables such as previous psychological distress and lack of a confiding relationship being more predictive of emotional difficulties following diagnosis (Pinder et al. 1994).

Each treatment is associated with emotional pressures of its own. For example, many people associate the radioactive substances used in radiotherapy with cancer, and fears about additional cancer being caused by the original treatment can be triggered as a result. Likewise, the nausea and vomiting associated with chemotherapy can become anticipated so strongly that the symptoms can start before the drugs are actually administered in a phenomenon called anticipatory nausea and vomiting. However, neither is associated with long-term increases in psychological problems (Hughson et al. 1986, 1987; Lee et al. 1992).

As mentioned earlier, ensuring patients receive a level of information appropriate to their needs can relieve unnecessary emotional suffering (Fallowfield et al. 1990). It has long been documented that other self-management strategies taught in preparation for unpleasant or painful procedures have a beneficial effect (see for example Egbert et al. 1964). Information combined with relaxation training prior to surgery has been shown to reduce the need for analgesics and the length of post-operative hospitalization (Anderson 1987).

Some interventions have explicitly attempted either to change the patient's perception of the demand of the anticipated event, or to increase their sense of being able to cope with it. These so-called cognitive interventions include distraction, focusing the attention elsewhere and using positive self-statements. A number of studies with dental patients and a variety of surgical patients have shown such strategies to be broadly helpful in reducing anxiety, pain and medication use and in reducing recovery times (Seyrek, Corah and Pace 1984; Wells et al. 1986; Ridgeway and Mathews 1982).

Surgery Surgery is useful for a number of reasons. It can be used to find out the primary site and type of cancer as part of the diagnostic procedures, for example through carrying out *biopsies* of internal organs. It can also be used to identify the stage of the cancer, for example by removing the lymph nodes adjacent to the site of disease. Once cancer has been confirmed, surgery may be used to remove solid tumours with a margin of surrounding normal tissue. Where cancer is causing symptoms such as pain or obstruction, surgery can be used as a palliative treatment in a procedure sometimes known as 'debulking'. Finally, it can be used as a reconstructive technique, for example following mastectomy in the case of breast cancer.

The emotional repercussions of surgery are multiple and are discussed in more detail in chapter 3. It may have an impact upon appearance or function, or a more subtle effect on self-image.

Albert was a 69-year-old widower who had major surgery as a result of a throat cancer. He had smoked a pipe all his life, and feared that this had been the cause of his disease. Earlier in his life he had tried to give up using his pipe at the request of his wife, but had never been successful. He experienced intense pain following his surgery, and although he was encouraged to discuss his needs for analgesia he refused. The nursing staff

were concerned that he seemed to be depressed, but the surgeons dis-
agreed as he was careful to show his gratitude to them for what he perceived as life-saving treatment. However, during one night shift, when a
nurse made a special effort to communicate with him (he had to write
down what he wanted to say) he indicated that he did not feel he deserved
to be free of pain as the cancer was his punishment for not breaking his
nicotine addiction.

Radiotherapy Again, radiation can be used both in diagnosis of cancer, for
example X-rays of bone metastases, and in its treatment. Initially the
treatment is planned, through the process of *simulation*, which involves meeting with a radiotherapist or clinical oncologist who works out the most
effective way to deliver the radiotherapy treatment. During this process, permanent tattoos are used to mark where the treatment is to be applied, and
these can act as a reminder after treatment has been completed. In the case
of a head or neck cancer a special mask is also made to help ensure the
accuracy of the treatment delivery. This can be a distressing experience in
itself, as the creation of the mask involves making an initial mould by cover-
ing the face.

   In the treatment of cancer, high-energy X-rays or gamma rays are used.
The aim of radiotherapy is to give as high a dose of radiation to the cancer
cells as possible, while preserving normal tissue. It is therefore given as a series
of bursts of radiation over a number of days or weeks, known as *fractions*, to
give the normal cells the best chance of surviving. As with surgery, one of the
advantages of radiotherapy is the localized effect of the treatment.

   Radiotherapy may be given externally or internally by inserting radioactive
sources into the body, for example in the case of some gynaecological cancers
when the effect of radiotherapy is maximized by delivering it through the
vagina. Progress is then reviewed weekly. The treatment itself is delivered by
radiographers. Radiotherapy can be used as a radical treatment in some
cases, in combination with other interventions, or to palliate symptoms, as in
the case of secondaries in the brain or bones.

   People receiving radiotherapy often have concerns about the risk of radiation poisoning.

John, a 62-year-old man, had been prescribed radiotherapy for a prostate
cancer. He was very fearful of the treatment, having witnessed the consequences for his mother. During his teens, his mother had been treated with

radiotherapy for breast cancer and subsequently developed leukaemia which he understood to be a direct result of her treatment. He was unaware of the developments in radiotherapy treatment that had significantly reduced the chances of such serious side effects, and so had not had the opportunity to alter his perception of the likelihood of a similar outcome for himself.

Chemotherapy Chemotherapy uses anti-cancer drugs (also known as *cyto-toxic drugs*) to destroy cancer cells. It is a *systemic* treatment carried around the body by the circulatory system and thus can reach all cancer cells. It is often used as an adjuvant treatment to surgery or in cancers that seem to be more widespread. The treatment can be taken orally, by injection or by infusion (sometimes through a central line directly into a larger blood vessel). Different drugs have different effects, and may be used in combination with each other. Treatment is usually given in cycles (sometimes over several months) to help to preserve normal cells in the body, which are quicker to repair themselves than the cancerous cells. Chemotherapy can be prescribed by clinical or medical oncologists, and is usually delivered by specialist nurses.

Side effects of chemotherapy, such as nausea, vomiting and hair loss, are well recognized. Improved pre-emptive medical management of the nausea and vomiting has made it an easier experience for many patients. However, there are those who are still affected and for some the symptoms develop in the period before receiving a dose of chemotherapy in what is known as anticipatory nausea and vomiting.

Bill, a 65-year-old man receiving chemotherapy for the treatment of meso-thelioma, a form of lung cancer, had become increasingly distressed during each cycle of chemotherapy. He had started to experience shortness of breath, accompanied by palpitations, just prior to and during the adminis-tration of the drugs and he was concerned that his disease was progressing. His nurse specialist discussed the situation with him, as she was finding it harder and harder to insert the needle that was required for the drugs to be given. Their conversation revealed that he had always been very fearful of needles and injections, and he was becoming anxious in anticipation of the needle being inserted. His shortness of breath and palpitations were a reflection of his anxiety, and they settled once the chemotherapy adminis-tration had finished. However, his interpretation of these symptoms was serving to increase his anxiety and so exacerbate the situation.

Hormonal therapies Naturally occurring chemical messengers can be used to treat some cancers that occur in those areas of the body usually regulated by hormones. They work by changing the hormonal environment and thus inhibit growth. An example is the use of tamoxifen tablets for women affected by breast cancer which is oestrogen-receptor-positive. The action of this drug is complex and not entirely understood, but it is believed that it may act as a replacement for naturally occurring oestrogen, blocking receptors on the surface of the cancer cell and thus restricting its growth. Like chemotherapy, hormonal therapies may be used as an adjunct to other treatments, such as surgery.

These treatments have wide-ranging side effects related to the usual actions of the hormones from which the treatments are derived. In the case of tamoxifen, women can experience side effects that mimic the symptoms of the menopause.

Jennifer, a woman in her early thirties who was taking tamoxifen as part of her treatment for breast cancer, started to experience hot flushes. Although she already had one young child, she and her husband had been trying to conceive at the point at which she was diagnosed with cancer. She became very distressed during the flushes, finding it hard to do anything and withdrawing from the world. She would become tearful and her thoughts would turn to the loss of her fertility and her consequent inability to have another child.

Biological therapies Research into the way the body responds to cancer has prompted attempts to find ways of assisting natural responses. Recent examples include Interleukin 2 and Interferon. Their mode of action is not fully understood, but they are thought to stimulate the body's own defence mechanisms. They may be delivered through injections, a cannula or a more a permanent line direct into a larger blood vessel. Side effects of these treatments include flu-like symptoms, fatigue and nausea.

Another exciting development is that of monoclonal antibodies such as herceptin and pallorex, which are currently the subject of clinical trials in the UK. Their mode of action is also not fully understood, but they appear to lock into proteins on the surface of the cancer cell, thus identifying it to the body's own immune system, which then destroys it. They are also being developed as a way of transporting radioactive and cytotoxic substances to the individual cancer cells in the body.

Transplants Bone-marrow transplants, and more recently stem-cell transplants, are primarily used in the treatment of haematological malignancies, such as leukaemia. The patient's own bone marrow is initially destroyed using chemotherapy drugs, in some circumstances with additional total body irradiation. The bone marrow or stem cells are then transplanted into them much as a blood transfusion is given. The bone marrow may have been harvested previously from the patient during remission, or from a relative or matched donor. Stem cells are generally harvested either from the patient or from the umbilical cord of new-born infants. This treatment is only available to those fit enough to cope with the demanding regime of chemotherapy and radiation required, and so generally only to patients under 50 years of age. The number of donors available from minority groups makes finding a matched unrelated donor for patients from minorities particularly difficult. There are a number of serious early and late complications which can make the procedure particularly complicated to manage. The measures required to prevent infection, including a period of isolation, can have a significant effect on the patient's mood.

Measuring treatment effectiveness During any course of treatment regular checks will be made on the response of the cancer. This might include scans or blood tests and the frequency varies depending on the treatment provided. Check-ups can be a source of great anxiety for those undergoing treatment. Patients can become acutely aware of changes in their body and worry about their significance in terms of disease progression. Many different variables are taken into account in estimating the effectiveness of treatments, including changes in the tumour size, changes in markers of tumour activity (such as serum CA 125 in the case of ovarian cancer), and symptoms as reported by the individual. Decisions about whether to continue to treat are based on such data.

Once treatment has been completed, patients may find the lack of appointments to attend and of active intervention difficult to adjust to. Many feel somewhat lost and isolated and their thoughts turn to the long term and what the experience means to them. They may be required to return regularly for check-ups, each of which can prompt worries to resurface about the possibility of recurrence.

Side effects Most treatments have some side effects, which may carry a great deal of significance for the patient. Physical side effects, such as the loss of hair associated with chemotherapy, also have a psychological component, signalling as they do that the person is unwell. Side effects may be either transient, or long-term, such as the absence of a breast after mastectomy or a stoma as a result of surgery on the bowel, for example. Other effects may be felt almost entirely on an emotional basis, with few outer signs. An example of this is the infertility of women who have been treated with certain chemotherapy regimes.

Management of Cancer which is beyond Hope of Cure

Cancer is responsible for a significant number of deaths in the UK. Lung cancer accounts for one quarter of these, and large bowel, breast and prostate cancer account for a further quarter (CRC 2000). In most of these cases there will be a period during which it is clear that treatment will not effect a cure, and instead the focus turns to managing the symptoms of advancing disease. Most of the investigations and treatments discussed above have their uses in the medical management of patients in the terminal phase of their disease. Surgery can be used to remove obstructions caused by the tumour, chemotherapy can be used to slow the spread, and short courses of radiotherapy can be used to reduce the pain associated with secondaries in the bones.

At this time, general physical symptoms, such as fatigue, can have a major impact on everyday life. Generally, the more advanced the disease is, the greater the level of distress. This may be due to the increasing burden of disease, the continued stress of treatments (as well as becoming more dependent upon others), the more immediate threat of death, or not being able to carry out important or enjoyable activities that make a significant contribution to well-being. Other particular challenges of advanced cancer can contribute to distress, including physical symptoms of increased pain, reduced appetite, weight loss and breathing difficulties, as well as concerns about more existential questions, such as whether there is life after death. Equally, patients may have concerns about the well-being of those they are leaving behind, and find it difficult to manage the distress of those around them.

Bill, the patient with mesothelioma we described earlier, was told by his oncologist that the chemotherapy he was receiving was not effective. Although Bill had known that his prognosis was not good, it came as a shock to him that his cancer was progressing as rapidly as it was. Bill's main concern was that his wife should be provided for in her widowhood. He became very anxious about the fact that a claim against his former employer, who he felt had been responsible for his exposure to substances linked to the development of mesothelioma, had not been resolved.

Bill's wife visited her general practitioner because she was upset that Bill was spending most of his time chasing people about his claim. He was left with little energy to enjoy time with his family, and she was resentful of the small amount of time he was spending with her as a result. Bill's GP referred the family to the local community palliative care service who were able to assist his wife in talking to Bill about her concerns.

Palliative care services and hospices provide a vital resource for people at all stages of cancer, even though they are perhaps most identified in the public's mind with advanced disease and terminal care. Their emphasis on symptom relief and promotion of well-being means that they are able to enhance the quality of life of patients and their carers. Community support can also be provided, along with access to solutions for practical problems associated with increased disability, such as equipment to assist with activities of daily living.

Conclusions

This chapter has outlined the key elements of the management of cancer and patients' experiences of it. We know that the nature of the disease and its treatment is not the whole story in explaining how people respond to cancer. The next chapter will explore this more fully and look at the processes that influence people's adjustment to cancer.

Summary

- Cancer is not one disease, but a collection of 200 diseases which share the ability to spread to other parts of the body through a process called metastasis.
- Lung, large bowel, prostate and breast cancers are the most common in adults and leukaemia in children. Each cancer differs in incidence and prevalence rates, as well as survival and mortality rates.
- Cancer is more common in the over-60s.
- Cancer patients experience many physical and emotional changes during their cancer journey.

- Initially patients may identify a symptom, possibly as a result of self-examination in the case of breast or testicular cancer, or as a result of a screening programme.
- Patients who have identified a symptom may delay presentation for a number of reasons, and onward referral may be delayed by health professionals at any point of the cancer journey.
- Screening programmes depend upon an identifiable and treatable pre-cancerous phase, but the individuals at highest risk may not attend.
- There are concerns about the emotional impact of screening, which is currently the subject of a number of studies.
- The period around diagnosis is a time of great uncertainty and high levels of distress. Patients generally want more information than they get, and effective management of information needs and participation in decision making can improve their psychological well-being.
- Preparation for procedures can improve patients' experiences of them, as well as reducing the amount of pain and recovery times.
- Treatments are varied and include surgery, chemotherapy, radio-therapy, hormone treatments and bone-marrow transplants, sometimes in combination, but different treatments are associated with particular difficulties, such as anticipatory nausea and vomiting in the case of chemotherapy.
- Monitoring treatment effectiveness and follow-up appointments can provoke a great deal of concern among patients, and fears of recurrence can encourage great attention to bodily changes.
- Advanced cancer is a time of high levels of distress, with additional general physical symptoms such as fatigue and loss of appetite. At this stage palliative care teams and hospice services have a great deal to offer in enhancing quality of life.

Chapter Three

The Impact of Cancer

There is no such thing as fact, only interpretation.
Niertzer, 17th century

A diagnosis of cancer gives rise to a set of problems which are specific to the individual receiving it. The nature and severity of these problems may fluctuate over time as the course of the disease unfolds and their impact will depend on many factors including:

- those related to the disease – including the nature and severity of the disease itself and any prescribed treatments;
- those related to the individual – including the way in which they construe life in general and cancer in particular;
- those related to environmental factors such as social support; and
- those related to the way in which health professionals interact with the individual concerned.

However, common to all individuals facing a diagnosis of cancer is the prospect of change and the need for physical, psychological and social adaptation to that change.

This chapter looks at the impact of cancer and the factors that influence it. It is divided into four sections as follows:

- the prevalence of psychological distress;
- the psychological and social impact of cancer (i.e. effects of diagnosis and treatment);
- individual responses to cancer (i.e. understanding adaptation);
- the role of the health care professional.

This framework will be used firstly to explore the notion and prevalence of psychological distress in cancer treatment and secondly to describe how psychosocial effects of cancer manifest themselves. Perhaps not surprisingly, clinicians have tended to focus on distress, but research has now highlighted the benefits of using a broader definition of well-being. The third section will therefore propose a model for understanding a person's individual response to cancer and the factors that influence it. The model is designed as a practical tool for carers and health professionals, whose role is to facilitate the optimum adaptation and well-being of their patients. The final section will highlight the role of health professionals in promoting well-being amongst their patients – a topic that is covered in more detail in chapters 6 and 7.

The Prevalence of Psychological Distress

Our understanding of distress has been shaped by what people have chosen to measure, with an emphasis on the concept of disorders. This has led to a focus in the research on the prevalence and detection of signs and symptoms, rather than seeing a continuum between well-being, distress and disorder. The diagnosis and treatment of cancer is clearly associated with high levels of psychological distress (Derogatis et al. 1983; Folkman and Greer 2000; Sellick and Crooks 1999). Although variations in the populations investigated, measures of psychological distress used and the point in the cancer journey at which the data are collected can make it difficult to compare research findings, there is now considerable evidence to suggest that between a quarter and a third of patients with cancer experience significant psychological distress. While it is not surprising that high levels of psychological distress exist amongst patients with cancer, a clearer idea of the extent of these problems is desirable to enable carers to mount an effective treatment response. This section therefore explores the prevalence of psychological distress and uses this information to challenge the approach currently adopted by many clinicians practising in this area.

Research indicates that people diagnosed with cancer have an increased risk of developing anxiety and depression. In fact, they are three times more likely to suffer from anxiety and depression than the general population and twice as likely as other medical patients. Meanwhile, available estimates of the prevalence of long-term psychological distress in cancer patients range from 20 per cent to 66 per cent (Derogatis et al. 1983, Parle et al. 1994).

While more research would help to refine the prevalence rate for long-term effects, the current figures already imply that there is something inherent to cancer and its treatments that is a risk factor for the development of psychological distress. Most of this distress shows up in the form of adjustment disorders such as anxiety and depression in the face of a stressful situation.

This leads to the obvious conclusion that anxiety and depression are a normal part of the process of adjustment and adaptation which takes place when people are diagnosed with and treated for cancer. The danger is that carers will zone in on the distress as being something that patients with cancer necessarily endure rather than developing ways to promote psychological well-being and discussing effective therapeutic treatments for anxiety and depression. Consider the parallel situation with physical pain: no one in this day and age would dismiss such pain as 'to be expected' and therefore with-hold analgesia. Before solutions can be explored, the distress must be identified.

Detection Despite the reported prevalence of distress, the emotional effects of cancer are seldom asked about in routine clinical settings. As a result, health professionals' rates of detecting people suffering with psychiatric disorders are notoriously low. Maguire (1984) reported detection levels of only between 20 per cent and 50 per cent. There is a similarly alarming disparity between the actual prevalence and rates of detection of the symptoms of distress. This is probably due to what has traditionally been a narrow and polarized view of a patient's emotional state; they are classified either as being 'OK' or else as suffering with a psychiatric disorder. This poses a dilemma for how cancer services regard and therefore respond to emotional effects. Where emotional issues are not routinely enquired about, the person with cancer is left thinking they are perhaps alone in feeling as they do. It also means that there is little prospect that a patient's reaction can be normalized in any way. Likewise, the labelling of displays of emotion as 'psychiatric disorders' can lead health professionals to avoid addressing them directly and opt instead for a referral to a counsellor, clinical psychologist or psychiatrist. Their reasons may include:

- fear that the patient may interpret such a line of inquiry as labelling them abnormal;
- fear of not being competent to deal with what they might uncover; and
- time constraints within busy clinics which can deter health professionals from asking about their patients' level of distress; patients, meanwhile, may be reluctant to raise the issue at all.

This presents a dilemma for both the patient and health professional. The patient is often left thinking that they are odd in some way for feeling the way they do. Likewise, the health professional can feel inhibited about discussing the patient's emotional distress. Acceptance of the existence of a continuum between well-being, distress and disorder, together with the ability and willingness to differentiate between them, is the first step in helping the patient adapt.

The Psychological and Social Impact of Cancer

A diagnosis of cancer is usually devastating for patients and their families. In coming to terms with their disease and its treatment, a person must deal not only with the threat to their survival, but also to likely changes to their lifestyle that will result from diagnosis and treatment. These include changes which impact on their family, social and work relationships. Not surprisingly, this is the kind of news that causes people to re-evaluate their lives and what is important to them. Concerns range from the everyday to the existential in the period following diagnosis (Weisman and Worden 1976–7). Health professionals do not always appreciate the need for patients to discuss the many aspects of their illness and in particular, the psychological effects of the disease and its treatment. This section looks at the psychological sequelae of diagnosis and treatment.

Psychological effects of diagnosis

While each person will experience their cancer differently, the psychological impact of it is reflected in changes in four areas:

- thoughts
- behaviour
- the body
- feelings.

Thoughts Unpleasant thoughts that cannot be easily put out of one's mind are likely to centre on events that have already happened, as well as anticipated.

> Following diagnosis, Sam found himself plagued with the thoughts: Will I be OK? Will I see my daughters grow up? Will I be able to work? These thoughts occurred frequently throughout the day and night and Sam found it extremely difficult to put them out of his mind. His thoughts centred around uncertainty and a lack of control.

Behavioural changes These may include disturbed sleep, tearfulness, being snappy or eating either less or more than usual.

> Following an episode of heavy bleeding, Susan had been admitted to hospital where she was diagnosed with cancer of the cervix.
>
> Susan started to check herself for any signs of bleeding whenever she went to the lavatory. This checking behaviour increased to the extent that she would go to the lavatory specifically to check for any bleeding. She also stopped going out for fear of not being able to find a lavatory where she could check herself. She found it difficult to get to sleep at night and described feeling tired, all of which made her more irritable causing arguments with her husband and children.

Bodily changes These may include breathlessness, palpitations, sweating, nausea and dizziness.

> Nick described feeling constantly on edge and panicky. This manifested itself as unpleasant somatic sensations including butterflies in his stomach and feeling sick, palpitations and breathlessness. These symptoms were worse at night and disrupted his sleep.

Feelings Typical feelings experienced include shock, disbelief and denial, fear and anxiety, anger and irritability, guilt, depression, hopelessness and helplessness.

> Susan had felt very shocked and frightened by the bleeding and her repeated thoughts about it happening again left her feeling threatened and anxious. This anxiety increased not only when she was unable to check herself but was also, paradoxically, maintained by her checking. She complained of feeling overwhelmed with fear and helpless to do anything about it. She also felt very guilty about being irritable and argumentative with her family.

In addition to the psychological effects of being diagnosed, many of the treatments for cancer can also have profound psychological consequences for patients.

Psychological effects of treatment

Surgery Surgery can involve the loss of a body part and/or loss of body function. Both can cause anxiety and depression as well as problems with body image and sexuality. Much of the research looking at the psychological impact of surgery has been carried out on breast and colorectal cancer patients. For patients with colorectal cancer, moderate to severe psychological distress is significantly higher in those who undergo colostomy, compared to those who have restorative surgery. However, in patients with breast cancer the incidence of psychological distress caused by conservative surgery (i.e. lumpectomy) versus radical surgery (i.e. mastectomy) is not significantly different (Fallowfield et al. 1990). It appears that the benefits of conservative treatment are negated in some women with breast cancer by concerns regarding cancerous cells being left behind. This suggests that the meaning of the outcome of surgery is a key factor in a person's resulting distress.

What does appear to be important in determining adjustment and well-being is patient participation in the choice of surgical treatment (Fallowfield 1990).

Radiotherapy There are a number of ways in which radiotherapy can be distressing for people with cancer. Preparation for radiotherapy can entail tattooing of the skin in order to ensure the accurate pinpointing of the area to be irradiated. This often causes distress to patients, as the tattoo serves as a permanent reminder of their disease.

> Jane recalled how the thought of being tattooed was awful. 'I felt like an animal being branded,' she said. 'I still get upset when I catch sight of the mark.'

For patients with head and neck cancer, the process of having a face mask made and its use during treatment can cause some to feel anxious and claustrophobic. The process of radiotherapy can also give rise to worries. Patients frequently report fear of damage, pain, burning and sterility as a result of the treatment itself (King et al. 1985). Moreover, a strong relationship between these adverse side effects occurring and subsequent anxiety and depression has been reported (Devlen et al. 1987).

Patients have reported feeling anxious at the prospect of radiotherapy postoperatively, as it can trigger worries about cancer cells having been left behind after surgery (Peck and Boland 1977).

Chemotherapy Chemotherapy has been associated with an increased risk of anxiety and depression. One in four patients experience nausea and vomiting, including anticipatory nausea (Morrow 1982). Side effects such as loss of hair and weight gain can give rise to body image problems, while loss of fertility can also cause sexual problems. Patients also frequently worry about the detrimental effects that the treatment may have on other healthy cells.

Hormonal treatments Hormonal treatments most commonly have an impact on a person's body image and sexual functioning, leading to significant distress. Side effects with which women may have to contend include the onset of menopause, weight gain, depression, growth of body hair and changes in voice tone. For men, side effects of treatment may include breast enlargement, weight gain, impotence and loss of sexual desire. All of these affect a person's sexual identity and sexuality.

Other treatments Stem-cell and bone-marrow transplants can give rise to anxiety concerning treatment-related mortality as well as concerns for the healthy donor. Long periods of isolation and restricted activity can also exacerbate mood problems.

> Catherine had been fully aware of the risks that a stem-cell transplant involved. During the course of injections aimed at boosting her white blood cells before harvesting them, Catherine had felt nervous but positive about her treatment. However, after the high-dose chemotherapy and transplant she became very depressed. She repeatedly worried whether she would succumb to an infection and found it difficult to differentiate between the side effects of the chemotherapy and symptoms of a possible infection. She did not discuss her worries with her family, for fear of upsetting them. Instead she constantly called staff for reassurance. This pattern of behaviour left her feeling disempowered and further worried about alienating staff.

Thus, treatment can have a marked impact on a person's psychological well-being. But to make matters more complicated, many of the symptoms of anxiety and depression mimic those of the disease, so it can be difficult to make sense of symptoms which potentially have a number of points of origin. This can lead to a vicious cycle where a patient can misinterpret their symptoms of distress as evidence of physical disease, triggering additional and unfounded anxiety.

Following the end of his treatment Mike was surprised to find himself feeling tired and with little energy. He had expected his energy levels to increase. Since stopping treatment he had begun to worry about the future and in particular whether to change jobs. He became convinced that his tiredness was due to his cancer and thought that it was indicative of the treatment having been unsuccessful. This thought made him anxious about his chances of survival and he experienced difficulty sleeping, which made him more tired and further fuelled his worries about his disease.

In a similar vein, patients can misconstrue physical symptoms as evidence of a psychological problem.

During her chemotherapy Kate became forgetful; she was unable to remember friends' names and had difficulty in finding the right word when speaking. She complained of having very poor concentration and described how her head was fuzzy. She thought she was 'going mad', but no one had told her that this could be a side effect of the treatment she was having.

This section has looked at some common psychological effects of cancer diagnosis and treatment. In summary, not only does the diagnosis of cancer cause psychological distress but also the prescribed treatments can be both physically and psychologically distressing. Many treatments have side effects, ranging from toxicity to loss of a body part or function. These are summarized in table 3.1.

People with cancer are, for the most part, ordinary people undergoing a stressful event for which they are often ill-prepared. It is to be expected that in the normal process of coming to terms with the demands that cancer and its treatments pose, people will experience emotional distress and, most notably, anxiety and depression. Up to a third of all patients will experience significant psychological distress.

The overlap of the physical disease and its symptoms with those of psychological distress has led researchers and clinicians to focus mainly on the prevalence and aetiology of distress. However, this reveals only part of the story as to how people adapt and adjust to illness. People also experience psychological well-being despite facing extremely difficult situations. Folkman and Greer (2000) argue that this aspect of a person's response to illness has been largely ignored by researchers. While overall levels of psychological distress tell us something of people with cancer generally, they tell us little about the processes by which individual patients experience and respond to their disease.

In this section we have suggested that this distress-focused approach creates

Table 3.1 Psychological effects of treatment

SURGERY	Anxiety
	Depression
	Body image
	Sexual problems
RADIOTHERAPY	Fatigue
	Nausea
CHEMOTHERAPY	Anxiety
	Depression
	Nausea *(incl. anticipatory)*
	Body image
	Fatigue
	Cognitive impairment
	(poor concentration, memory loss)
HORMONAL	Anxiety
	Depression
	Body image
	Sexual problems

an artificial divide between the psychologically 'healthy' and 'unhealthy', which obscures the importance of trying to enhance the psychological well-being of anyone with cancer. It also risks over-pathologizing what are commonplace symptoms, which can have the knock-on effect of causing patients to feel stigmatized and staff to distance themselves from asking about this distress. This in itself can prevent patients and staff from beginning to address how to deal with these symptoms and reduce distress and promote well-being.

The next section introduces a model that explores the myriad factors that influence the meaning a person attributes to their cancer and situation, thereby laying the foundations for developing a more holistic approach to an individual's cancer treatment.

Individual Responses to Cancer: Understanding Adaptation

People operate by developing a model of their world. This is a normal and ongoing process allowing individuals to make sense of demands made of them and respond accordingly. In short, they adapt. For example, a pain in the stomach following a large meal will be given a different meaning to one that comes on suddenly for no apparent reason. These different responses are due to the interpretation of the stomach pain. Central to this process of adaptation are two processes:

- appraisal
- coping.

Figure 3.1 clearly illustrates the various stages involved in responding to the stress or change that cancer and its treatment represents (Parle and Maguire 1995 after Lazarus and Folkman 1984).

When faced with a diagnosis of cancer and its possible treatments (demand) a person will attempt to make sense of the situation (primary appraisal) and then weigh up their response options (secondary appraisal). On the basis of these appraisals, the individual will select a strategy for coping. Lazarus and Folkman's model refers to this as the coping response. This response com-

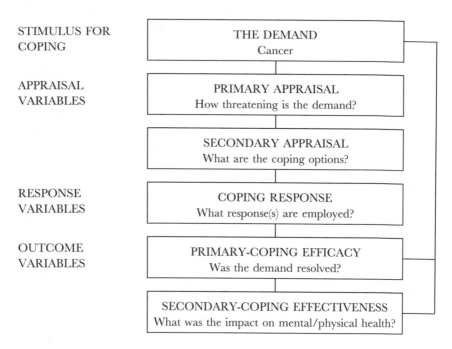

STIMULUS FOR
COPING

THE DEMAND
Cancer

APPRAISAL
VARIABLES

PRIMARY APPRAISAL
How threatening is the demand?

SECONDARY APPRAISAL
What are the coping options?

RESPONSE
VARIABLES

COPING RESPONSE
What response(s) are employed?

OUTCOME
VARIABLES

PRIMARY-COPING EFFICACY
Was the demand resolved?

SECONDARY-COPING EFFECTIVENESS
What was the impact on mental/physical health?

Figure 3.1   *Variables associated with different models of coping*

prises the behaviour and thoughts a person employs to control their distress (emotion-focused coping) and the actual response that they mount (problem-focused coping) to deal with the original demand or event. The outcome of the coping response is thus as much a function of how the person feels emotionally as how they behave in the face of the situation.

> Following the removal of a testicle, Robert described feeling inadequate as a man and unable to contemplate having a sexual relationship with a woman ever again. Understandably his sense of loss and anticipated loss made him feel sad and depressed.

The same loss in an older widower may be accepted philosophically and so give rise to less distress. This demonstrates that the appraisal or meaning ascribed to an event, rather than the event itself, is key in determining a person's response. It follows that as well as understanding the processes involved in adaptation, health professionals must also be aware of the factors that influence meaning. These so-called mediating factors have been researched and together can explain why people feel and behave as they do.

In the next section these factors are listed and their relationship to the processes involved in the model of adaptation explored.

Mediating factors

These are the factors which form the context within which individuals make sense of their cancer and determine their adaptation to it. They comprise both psychological and environmental and social factors. Psychological factors pertain to the person themselves, for example personality, previous history of psychological difficulties, and how they view their illness and its outcome. Environmental and social factors, meanwhile, refer to the person's social environment. These include cultural beliefs about cancer and previous experience of cancer, social support and life events.

Psychological factors

Personality Personality can be defined as the dispositional variables that influence how a person thinks about and responds to demands or stressors in life. It is the psychological signature of the individual, defined by the interaction of their genetic predisposition and their life experiences. Appraisal is influenced by personality. People who are inclined to worry may become more preoccupied and anxious about their symptoms, and more likely to interpret them as signalling serious illness or death. This is known as catastrophizing. In other words, their primary appraisal of their symptoms is that they represent a potential threat. They are also more likely to think that there is little they can do to control the situation (secondary appraisal). As a result of this catastrophizing, their anxiety increases.

Felicity described her reaction.
'When I discovered the lump I automatically thought the worst. I was convinced that it was cancer, and put off going to my GP because I was so scared of what he might find. I saw my life coming to an end and I kept thinking of my children and what I'd say to them. It was awful. I didn't sleep for weeks.'

Following his treatment for non-Hodgkin's lymphoma, Ben, who was married with two young children, suffered with nightmares and intrusive thoughts about the prospect of not seeing his children grow up. He spent increasing amounts of time during the day focusing on his physical symptoms which had the effect of making him less inclined to go to the park and play with the children.

Research has indicated optimism, mastery and internal locus of control as being personality traits that positively influence a person's appraisal of stressors. By contrast, individuals who are inclined to low, depressed mood tend to interpret their misfortunes as a personal failing, attributing blame to themselves. They also tend to see the future as hopeless and significant others as likely to abandon them. As a result of this tendency to appraise events negatively they are likely to perceive cancer as representing a loss that is out of their control.

Charles recalled his reaction to his testicular cancer and chemotherapy.
'It's strange but I've often thought I wouldn't be able to have children, and I probably won't now. Bang goes any thought of Jemma marrying me. She is mad on children.'

On one level, Helen – who always believed herself to be unlucky – was not surprised to be diagnosed with breast cancer. With no nodal involvement the prognosis was good. However, she could not shake the belief that she would be part of the 50 per cent of people that would not survive five years.

Individuals who are suspicious of others can become concerned about the trustworthiness of people caring for them, attributing to them hostile intentions and a systematic disregard for their rights. People commonly try to make sense of the events that happen to them. The way they look at the world will naturally influence their appraisal of present-day situations. All of these influences shape the meaning an individual gives to their situation and their attempts to adapt to it.

Coping response Coping is the response or strategy a person mounts to deal with a particular demand, either through ways of thinking and feeling or by taking action. Greer et al. (1979) identified a number of 'coping styles' in women with breast cancer. These have been modified in the light of more recent research (Watson et al. 1994). A full description of these can be found in *Counselling People With Cancer* (Burton and Watson 1998). A criticism of the notion of coping style, as opposed to that of coping strategy, is that it implies a stable response over time. In reality of course, patients will exhibit many coping strategies and can be taught alternative strategies. That said, certain coping strategies have been associated with better psychological outcome. Some studies have emphasized the advantages of active rather than passive or avoidant coping strategies. Take the example of the coping strategy known as 'fighting spirit'. Here the patient tends to view the cancer as a challenge, assumes that successful strategies are available and feels able to implement them. While the goals may vary over time, from cure to good quality of life in the palliative phase, the patient takes control over what is judged possible to influence, without wasting energy on strategies or goals that are worthless.

> Nikki had been diagnosed with bone metastases and had been told that she had up to one year to live. She resolved to make the best use of this 'precious resource', and booked the trip to Australia that she and her husband had been promising themselves for many years.

The use of avoidance may be less anxiety-provoking than more active information-seeking strategies, at least in the acute phases of diagnosis and treatment (Watson et al. 1984). What this suggests is that people use different coping strategies at different times during their illness and the following section illustrates these.

The research into how coping relates to psychological and disease outcome has been fraught with methodological problems. Many of the research findings are not comparable as they use different definitions of coping. In particular, confusion exists as to whether coping refers to the appraisal of the stressful situation, the elicited response or a combination of the two. (See Parle and Maguire 1994 for further discussion of coping.)

Beliefs about illness In an attempt to understand their symptoms, people develop internal representations of their illness: what it means to them, the cause, duration, prognosis and what they think can be done about it (Leventhal et al. 1980). These are formed on the basis of the person's knowledge, attitudes, beliefs, expectations and predictions about their illness. Eliciting a person's views of their illness or illness representation is important, as these have been found to account for much of the variation in people's adjustment to illness.

Dave believed that his stomach cancer was entirely due to genetic influences and that there was little he could do now to alter the outcome. His father had been diagnosed with cancer of the stomach at a similar age and lived for many years afterwards. Dave did not see any real benefit in changing his lifestyle and eating habits.

After being diagnosed with early-stage breast cancer, Isabel was frightened that she would die as her sister had done twenty years previously from a different and invasive breast cancer.

A diagnosis of cancer can invalidate a person's general model of the world. On receiving their diagnosis, people often talk about their world having fallen apart.

Maria had always thought of herself as lucky, but when she was diagnosed with cancer she found it difficult to reconcile this with her previous outlook on life.

'I feel as though my luck's run out and I'm now in the land of the sick and don't know how to get out.'

Beliefs about a person's illness are important in their adaptation, as they determine a person's interpretation (appraisal) and coping response to their situation.

History of psychological difficulties How a person has responded to difficulties previously can be helpful in predicting how they will adjust to cancer. It is helpful to know how a patient has dealt with change and loss in the past, and whether they have had any psychological difficulties in the past.

Asking about a person's previous coping also gives insight into strengths and potential vulnerabilities. The notion of self-efficacy is important here. This is the belief a person has that not only is there a solution but that they can implement that solution. It is helpful to know whether the cancer has reignited earlier issues which may be unresolved, such as the death of a loved one, as this can affect their adjustment.

Environmental factors

Cultural influences Cancer is a commonly feared disease. There is a perception both that it is a modern disease and that it is increasing. Cancer is most commonly associated with death, people referring to it as 'the big C' and 'a death sentence'. In fact, as explained in the previous chapter, cancer covers a multitude of differing diseases that have been around for many thousands of years and have varying prognoses.

Although cancer is a disease that is a great deal more likely to affect people in old age, it is nevertheless feared by young and old alike. This apparent discrepancy can perhaps be explained by changes in the social management of death and dying which have taken place in the twentieth century. Whereas deaths often used to take place in the person's home, with family and friends in attendance, this is now less likely to be the case. It is now more common for people to die in hospital or other institutions. In addition, practices such as having the body at home for the period prior to the funeral are less common. Hence, people have little direct experience of death and dying and as a result these have become more remote and so more feared.

In such situations, taboos typically develop. Taboos are beliefs intended to protect from or defend against the anxieties that illness, dying and death raise. They extend to other sensitive issues, such as sexual behaviour, and often result in their avoidance in conversation or even denial of their existence altogether. In the Western world, youth, health and beauty are revered and this adds to the fear of becoming old, ill and seemingly unattractive.

As individuals living within societies, we adopt or internalize these taboos. Hence, people often feel a sense of blame and guilt for having developed cancer. 'Why me?' is a question with which people struggle to come to terms. Unaffected individuals and society at large contribute to this sense of self-blame by distancing themselves from the frightening but inevitable prospect of illness and death via a set of beliefs or myths that allows them to regard people with cancer as different from themselves. How often do we hear people comment, 'He didn't look after himself', or 'She smoked', the implication being that something about the person caused their cancer.

Lillian, a 40-year-old woman, was diagnosed with ovarian cancer shortly after she had left a religious community. She subsequently became worried that leaving the community had caused her cancer and that others would see it as a 'punishment' for her act. This triggered thoughts of guilt and self-blame, which in turn left her feeling overwhelmed and depressed about the course of her disease and her ability to influence it. As a result, she initially declined treatment, which she believed would not help her. This strategy enabled her to avoid difficult and upsetting feelings by allowing her to continue life apparently unaffected. However, it also precluded her from making informed choices about her future and denied her the chance to receive effective treatments.

Cultural beliefs and taboos affect individuals in a number of ways. In general, avoiding feared situations has the effect of increasing the fear associated with them. By using avoidance the person reduces their anxiety, because they are not putting themselves in the feared situation. However, such avoidance precludes the individual from ever developing alternative strategies or responses for dealing with their anxiety. This has a knock-on effect for what Lazarus and Folkman (1984) identify in their model as secondary appraisal, that is, the belief that one can do something about the situation. Therefore, in the long term, avoidance maintains and increases fear.

Clinically, cultural beliefs and taboos are important factors in determining what are referred to as health-related behaviours, such as advice seeking and adherence to treatments. Take for example certain religious groups who regard blood transfusions as unacceptable. Such beliefs will directly influence a patient's decision to have or sustain chemotherapy, with its risk of neutrapenia and subsequent blood transfusion. Similarly, in cultures where fertility is of paramount importance to a person's social standing, patients may decline treatment options that threaten their fertility. Possibly the taboos surrounding having cancer prevent some people from acknowledging their symptoms, the end result being avoidance in the shape of delay in seeking medical advice.

The number of euphemisms used to describe cancer in a language is also an indication of how culturally we avoid the word cancer. Cyst, mole, tumour and growth are all words that are used to refer to the disease. Meanwhile the word cancer itself has entered everyday language to describe unpleasant experiences. For example, corruption in organizations is often described as 'a cancer'. As a result, practices such as avoiding informing people of their true diagnosis have taken hold at various periods in time. Only in the last twenty years have patients been routinely informed of their cancer diagnosis. Interestingly, much of the research into the psychological effects of cancer focused on breast cancer for the sole reason that patients with breast cancer, unlike other patients with cancer, were told of their diagnosis. The reason for this was that their permission was needed for the radical and visible surgery mastectomy entailed.

Social support There is a good deal of evidence to indicate that good social support and a confiding relationship have a positive effect on physical and emotional health. Where a person's social support provides emotional support and the opportunity to openly discuss and resolve difficulties, it acts as a buffer against psychological problems. Likewise where the quality of social support is poor, it can exacerbate the problems associated with cancer. Effective social support may improve survival. Speigel (1985) has reported a significant increase in longevity amongst women with metastatic breast cancer attending a psychosocial support group. The presence of a confiding relationship has also been found to affect advice-seeking behaviour. In one study it has been observed that women were six times more likely to delay their presentation with breast cancer if they did not share the discovery of their symptoms with someone else within a few days (Burgess et al. 1998). Low socio-economic status is also a factor which increases the risk of emotional difficulties during times of stress (Brown and Harris 1978).

Life events A previous negative experience of cancer in the family can adversely affect a patient's adjustment to their own cancer. There is evidence in the general population that a high number of stressful events can adversely affect a person's ability to cope with future demands.

Role of the Health Professional in Promoting Psychological Well-being

There are many ways in which health professionals can enhance a patient's well-being. Earlier in this chapter we saw that the key factors in predicting a good outcome and coping include:

- the patient being able to view the demand as a challenge rather than as a threat or loss;
- a belief by the patient in his ability to do something to control the situation;
- an ability to define priorities, set goals and solve problems.

It may be unrealistic to expect a health professional to swim against the tide of the many factors which shape someone's initial appraisal of their situation. There may be more opportunity, however, to help shape a patient's sense that something can be done about the situation and that they can contribute to this. Health professionals can help people adapt in a variety of ways. These include:

- broadening the scope of the caring relationship to include what matters most to the individual patient as well as the issues which are most pressing to the health professional;
- providing information about both the nature of the clinical challenge to be faced and the strategies which can be adopted to deal with it;
- being instrumental in helping patients access the informational, practical and emotional support they require to tackle problems as they see them.

The earlier chapters of this book had a twofold aim:

1   to help health professionals step into the shoes of their patients' psychological experience of having cancer; and
2   to better understand the factors which contribute to that experience.

The object of the remaining chapters of the book is to help health professionals understand the valuable contribution they can make to the psychological well-being of their patients (Folkman and Greer 2000).

We have ended this chapter by alluding to the processes involved in this and will elaborate these in chapters 4 and 5.

Summary

- A diagnosis of cancer is associated with high levels of psychological distress.
- Between a quarter and a third of cancer patients experience significant psychological distress.
- Patients with cancer are three times more likely to suffer from anxiety and depression than the general population and twice as likely as other medical patients.

- Prescribed treatments can be both physically and psychologically distressing.
- Side effects range from toxicity to loss of a body part or function.
- Some side effects mimic aspects of anxiety and depression which can exacerbate psychological problems during treatment.
- While each person will experience their cancer differently, the psychological impact is reflected in changes in four main areas: thoughts, behavioural changes, bodily changes and feelings.
- Researchers and clinicians have tended to focus on the prevalence and aetiology of distress rather than promoting a model of psychological well-being. This has led to an unhelpful notion of the psychologically healthy and unhealthy patient.
- Folkman and Greer's model describes the two core processes (appraisal and coping) which contribute to well-being and what health care professionals can do to facilitate this in patients with cancer.
- People operate by developing a model of their world. Their response to cancer is affected in turn by a wide range of psychological and environmental mediating factors.
- Certain coping responses have been associated with better psychological outcome, with studies emphasizing the advantages of active rather than passive or avoidant coping strategies.
- Key predictors of well-being include:
  - the patient construing a particular demand as a challenge rather than a threat or loss;
  - a belief by the patient in his ability to do something to exert control over the situation;
  - an ability to identify priorities, set goals and solve problems.
- Despite high levels of reported distress, the emotional effects of cancer are seldom routinely asked about in clinical settings. Health professionals have an important role to play and can significantly enhance the psychological well-being of their patients through:
  - eliciting what the core issues are for their patient, providing information about the clinical challenge facing the patient and discussing strategies that could help them;
  - focusing on what can change and establishing clear goals with the patient;
  - helping patients access the informational, practical, social and emotional support they need to deal with problems.

Chapter Four

The Helping Process

Health professionals aim to help those facing a health problem towards greater well-being. This is achieved through a helping process, including identifying and tackling health-related problems. The helping process is facilitated by the relationship between the helper and the patient. This chapter will look at the nature of the helping relationship between patients and health professionals, the factors that affect it and the process of helping itself. The actual skills required to develop the helping relationship and work through the process will be explored in chapter 5.

What is a Helping Relationship?

In the past, health professionals have generally been cast as experts, often developing rather paternalistic relationships with patients as a result. In such a situation, the views of the patient matter little, as the professional defines and holds the key to the problems to be addressed. However, modern understanding of how people respond to ill-health has revealed the patient to be an active influence. This has prompted the reconsideration of the role of the health professional. The health professional and the patient are now more realistically seen as adults in an equal relationship, which we will call the helping relationship. The patient is actively involved in the decision-making process. The health professional helps the patient negotiate the challenges that cancer brings by taking on a more advisory role and offering information and choices for the patient to consider.

Patients appreciate being active partners in their health care, and the collaborative helping relationships we will be describing in this chapter contribute towards their being able to achieve this. As a result they feel cared for and respected by health professionals, as well as appreciating the chance to be an equal in finding solutions to what is, after all, their problem.

Egan (1998) proposed that in their helping relationships with patients, health professionals act as consultants. They participate in a relationship with the person who is seeking resolution of a problem, but they do not take over responsibility. They will, therefore, listen, teach, challenge, support and advise, and provide technical expertise (diagnosis and treatment), but ultimately the patient retains responsibility for the situation. This should not, however, be seen as a bid to transform patients into consumers, responsible for picking a treatment of their own choosing from a shelf. It is rather about a partnership in which the professional and patient share in the process of dealing with the patient's health and associated problems.

Before exploring how the helping relationship can be used with patients, let us first examine what determines the quality of it.

Factors which Affect the Helping Relationship

There are a wide range of factors that can facilitate or impede the helping relationship. These factors can be grouped under three headings: the setting, health professional factors and patient factors. Although it is possible to group them thus, it should not detract from the fact that they all interact. For example a professional may believe that asking about feelings will cause undue distress in the patient. Thus cues of distress, such as crying, from the patient may be overlooked or avoided. The patient may interpret this as meaning that distress is not an appropriate topic to raise, and in subsequent interviews try to cover it up.

In this section we will explore some of the relevant issues, particularly those underlying the basic conditions necessary for a good relationship and, given the emphasis on beliefs as a mediator of emotions and behaviours, the beliefs of those involved in the relationship. Some of the factors identified are drawn from general research about helping relationships, while others are specific to what is known about communication with people about cancer. Later in the book we will discuss how to manage these factors when seeing patients.

The setting

Patients who are unfamiliar with the environment and perhaps anxious about what is happening to them can be very alert to what is going on around them. What they see, hear or experience can all be used as evidence in their attempt to make sense of what is happening to them. There are many aspects of the health setting that can thus affect the helping relationship. Firstly, the general condition of the environment is important; for example graffiti on the walls and broken chairs may be interpreted by the patient as meaning they are not valued by the service they are using. The lack of a private place can make it hard for the patient to talk about upsetting or embarrassing topics. Being interrupted by the telephone or by other people coming into the room can disrupt the flow of thought and conversation, and reduce a patient's willingness to share something that is troubling them. These aspects of the setting potentially affect the breadth and depth of information that the health professional is likely to receive from the patient, by making the latter reluctant to disclose information before the interview has even begun. These factors might also make it harder for the health professional to get across complex information to the patient who is more likely to be relaxed and attentive when seen in private with no interruptions.

More subtle aspects of the setting are also important, such as the furniture. Chairs of different heights can exacerbate the sense that the relationship is unequal, particularly when the patient is seated lower than the professional. This rather obviously reflects the more paternalistic approach that we are trying to replace. Furniture, such as a desk, can also act as a barrier between the professional and the patient. Again these aspects of the setting can make patients more reluctant to talk openly, and so opportunities to understand and help them can be lost.

The health professional

The behaviours displayed by health professionals have a significant impact on how patients think and feel about the relationship. Health professionals' beliefs and emotional state are important predictors of that behaviour, and so we will examine salient issues related to all three factors.

Beliefs There are two main sorts of relevant beliefs: about the professional's role (including what they are responsible for, and their competence to deal with issues), and about the patients and their role (such as their activity or passivity in the relationship).

Beliefs about their role in the helping relationship are often a reflection of the professional's specific pre-qualification training and subsequent training. Professionals are commonly taught that their role is to identify medical signs and symptoms and provide solutions to them. They may, therefore, pay selective attention only to those patient cues that are relevant to this role. A doctor may respond to the report of pain rather than the worry expressed about its meaning. They may also try to provide a solution to the first issue identified rather than continue to explore what other concerns may be present. It is possible that the issue raised is not the most important, but gets most time by virtue of being discussed first. In addition, there may be insufficient time available to elicit other concerns, or the patient may forget them until after they leave.

Professionals' beliefs about their competence to deal with a particular issue can have a strong effect on how they respond. Many health professionals are lacking in confidence to discuss emotional matters with their patients, and so distance themselves when the patient gives a cue about distress. This can be expressed as changing the topic of discussion or giving immediate reassurance, for example telling a crying patient it is natural to feel distressed, and continuing without exploring the nature of the distress any further. This can extend to the belief that by paying attention to the broader concerns of the patient, rather than confining discussions to the medical details, a 'can of worms' may be opened and the consequences become unmanageable.

Professionals often have important beliefs about the consequences of changing their clinical practice, or about predictions that can lead them to avoid any changes. For example they might believe that allowing the patient to contribute to setting the agenda will be detrimental both to the patient and to themselves, and that it will lead to more time being required for a consultation or other important medical issues being missed. Professionals may predict that the cumulative effects of dealing with a number of patients in that way would mean that clinics would overrun. The worst-case scenario sees a professional overwhelmed by the huge numbers of problems brought up by the patient. As a result the consultation runs over time as the patient becomes increasingly distraught, eventually leaving the interview no better off, or even worse than they were at the start.

Beliefs about and attitudes towards patients are also important. These may include the degree to which the health professional expects the patient to be active or passive in the relationship, or the degree to which the patient is expected to modify his or her lifestyle significantly. Health professionals who believe that they are responsible for decision making about treatment may find it difficult to deal with a patient who arrives at the consultation with a sheaf of papers about treatments that they have found on the internet. Equally, those health professionals who have a firm belief that people with smoking-related diseases ought to stop smoking may become exasperated by the patient who has shortness of breath, yet still smokes forty cigarettes each day.

Beliefs that are helpful in the health care relationship are also characteristic of any effective relationship. These include believing the patient to be worthy of your respect, value and genuine interest. These ideas are somewhat similar to Rogers's (1957) conditions for therapeutic personality change. They form the bedrock of the helping relationship. When the patient feels that their helper has these attitudes towards them, rapport is established, and a working alliance formed. The three most important attitudes are summarized below.

Empathy This involves attempting to understand the world from the point of view of the patient. In the same way that professionals are constantly forming views about the presenting problem, developing management strategies and testing them out, so is the patient trying to understand and manage the situation. An empathetic attitude allows the health professional to understand the concerns of their patients and helps them to focus on what really matters to the patient. Patients who feel that their problem has not been fully appreciated will be harder to engage and work with. There is always the dilemma of how to reconcile potentially differing views of the problem. It is almost always more easily managed when the professional is able to demonstrate an understanding of the patient's own view of their situation as well as explaining their own.

Respect This is a fundamental part of all functional relationships, in the health care setting as in any other. Respect involves valuing the person and not sitting in judgement. Most simply, it is demonstrated by taking the time to introduce yourself, giving your full attention and allowing sufficient time for the patient's contribution to the consultation. Such simple measures allow patients to feel a part of the relationship, and they are therefore likely to respond more favourably to it.

It is also demonstrated by conveying to patients that they are accepted regardless of their decisions and choices. This may at times be challenging – exasperation in the face of people with lung cancer who continue smoking may be a natural reaction. However, patients need to be assured that such feelings are directed at their behaviour rather than about them fundamentally.

Genuineness Being genuine in one's relationships is essentially being oneself when interacting with others. People who are at home with themselves are genuine in their interactions with others, including their patients. This might include admitting the limits of skill or expertise, admitting when one does not know the answer and being prepared to acknowledge how one's own personal opinions influence one's practice. The health professional exhibits genuineness in his interactions when he is truly interested in the patient as a person and is not just trying to live up to professional roles. It implies honesty and integrity in professional practice.

The following is an excerpt from the opening few moments of a discussion between a radiographer and her patient, who was coming to receive a fraction of radiation after a weekend away. The radiographer in this situation demonstrates towards her patient all of the fundamental attitudes that are the hallmarks of effective communication.

Cathy: Good morning, Mr Jones. How have you been over the weekend?

Mr Jones: Well, OK I suppose.

Cathy: It sounds as though something is on your mind. Would you like to tell me about it?

Mr Jones: Well, actually, I'm fed up with this radiotherapy. It's making my skin really sore.

Cathy: I'm really sorry to hear that, Mr Jones. I'm very aware that sometimes people's skin does get sore in the site that they are having their radiotherapy. Perhaps I could have a look at it in a moment to see if there is anything we can do to help with that. Is the sore skin causing any particular sorts of difficulties for you?

Mr Jones: It's waking me up at night, when I roll onto that side. I'm getting really irritable – my wife says I'm like a bear with a sore head!

Cathy: So not only is the skin sore, but it's disturbing your sleep and making you irritable. Have I got that right? You can hardly have been looking forward to coming back for more today then. Is there anything else that has been on your mind?

In this case Cathy, the radiographer, gets the discussion off to a good start by saying hello and enquiring how her patient was before continuing with what is on her agenda – delivering the radiotherapy. She makes sure that she checks out the reasons for his rather downbeat response to her enquiries, and is not defensive when he highlights his problems with the treatment she has been delivering to him. Rather than just dealing with the first problem raised, she then goes on to summarize what he has said, checking with him that she has been understood accurately. Finally, she prompts him to raise any other difficulties he is experiencing. Throughout this Mr Jones is likely to feel that Cathy is truly interested in what has been happening to him and values trying to help him with it. As a result, as well as finding a solution to these difficulties, Mr Jones is more likely to raise concerns with Cathy in the future and to feel that he has an ally.

Emotions The health professional's emotional state can also affect the help-ing relationship. Working with people with health problems is often stressful work and many show signs of burnout. Over time professionals can come to feel exhausted and cut off from their patients. Again this acts as a trigger to block picking up patients' concerns in order to avoid being overwhelmed by the demands of the work. Professionals' motivation for working in this area is often to help people, and they may take responsibility upon themselves for solving all the patients' problems.

> A young hospital doctor, Rashid, found it distressing to hear that her patient, John, was having difficulties with nausea and vomiting because of the chemotherapy he was receiving. Despite attempts to control the symp-toms they were intractable, and Rashid started to think that this was a reflection on her professional capabilities. She avoided visiting John in order to avoid the painful feelings that these thoughts provoked.

Acknowledging that the health professional is but one partner in the situation, able to take responsibility for delivering solutions to only some parts of the problem, can help with such thoughts and feelings.

Behaviours The behaviours displayed by health professionals are a reflec-tion of their beliefs and emotional state, and can have a significant effect on the helping relationship. Distancing from the patient because of burnout might be demonstrated by health professionals failing to introduce themselves. They may make minimal eye contact, which may be interpreted by the patient as being a sign that they are untrustworthy. Perhaps most importantly, health professionals' beliefs about the appropriateness of discussing emotional mat-ters may mean they never enquire about them. Patients can conclude quite early in the relationship that it is, therefore, an area of their life not to be discussed.

Some behaviours of health professionals can have an unintended detrimen-tal impact. In some cases continuing private conversations in front of patients may be interpreted by the patient as an indication that their own problem is second on the list of priorities, which may make the patient feel isolated. The content of such discussions can also be anxiety-provoking for the patient, who might overhear words they do not understand or which alarm them. A pa-tient undergoing a biopsy overheard two surgeons discussing the morning theatre list, during which they commented that people are silly to delay seeing their general practitioner about an obviously worrying symptom as it might worsen their prognosis. The patient took this to mean that he had left it too late to seek help, and so was likely to die from a skin cancer.

The patient

Given that the helping relationship by definition involves two parties, it is clear that the patient's beliefs, emotional state and behaviours are also highly influential. However, their physical state can also be important, particularly when they have active disease.

Beliefs Patients may have a number of salient beliefs about the health professionals they deal with. Their age, gender or race may be pertinent to the patient's expectations of treatment; for example they may think that someone is too young to have the necessary experience to deliver effective treatment. They may believe that it is inappropriate to discuss sensitive issues with someone younger than themselves, or, for that matter, older than them, or of a different gender or culture. At the extreme, this can extend to prejudice of any sort.

Professionals are often seen as busy with other important demands on their time. This belief can result in reluctance to raise concerns. The exposure given to some research about the possibility of positive attitude impacting on survival can lead patients to believe that they should not express distress. Again, this can reduce the chances that they will discuss it with a professional unless they are specifically asked.

Emotions The emotional state of the patient will also affect their participation in the relationship. Cancer is generally a threatening disease, and the frequent potential for bad news can result in the flight-or-fight response being triggered. This can reduce the patient's capacity to attend and concentrate, and may make them more irritable than usual. Some experiences induce reactions similar to those experienced by survivors of traumas, making them vigilant to cues in the environment that suggest they may exposed to a threat, such as more bad news. They may be particularly sensitive to cues displayed by the professional, such as appearing nervous, and try to fit them into their understanding of the situation, in this case that of a threat. Thus emotional state has a big influence on the way patients think during clinical interviews and what they remember about them afterwards.

Behaviour Equally, just as the health professional's beliefs and emotions influence their behaviour in the helping relationship, the same happens with patients. Fear about the possibility of bad news may lead to avoidance of appointments showing itself as persistent lateness. Patients may also show irritable behaviour, being short-tempered or snappy, as a reflection of underlying concern or anger.

Physical state Finally, the physical state of the patient can have a bearing on how the relationship is established and maintained. Patients who are acutely unwell may be easily fatigued, in pain or find it hard to concentrate. These factors make it difficult for them to follow and take part in conversations. Practical strategies, such as limiting the length of consultation, encouraging the patient to have someone with them for the meeting and backing it up with written information can all help to offset these difficulties.

In this section we have briefly touched on the factors that may influence the helping relationship. Of these, we have perhaps focused most on beliefs as a key variable affecting both emotional and behavioural reactions to situations. The importance of the beliefs of both the health professional and the patient lies in the way in which they reciprocally influence the response of both to the process. They may interact in a helpful or unhelpful way. For example, a health professional with a strong belief in the patient making treatment decisions for themselves may find it harder to manage the care of a patient who believes the doctor should make the decision because they are the expert. Both sets of beliefs affect the way in which the patient is investigated and treated. If the patient believes a symptom to be unimportant and so does not report it, the health professional cannot take it into account in choosing between different management strategies. Likewise, a health professional who believes a particular patient would become very distressed if told the truth about a poor prognosis, may be unrealistically upbeat in their discussions with them. This may prevent the patient from having the opportunity to address any issues concerning impending death, such as saying goodbye to significant people.

The Process of Helping

In the first part of this chapter we explored the relationship between professionals and patients. This might be thought of as the vehicle, whereas the process of helping is the route map to be followed during interviews. The purpose of this final section is to explain the stages involved, and we will then go on to explore the skills involved in the next chapter.

The aims of the helping process, as Egan (1998) sees it, are to enable people to identify and manage their own problems. He describes the process of helping as initially exploring the problem, then developing new perspectives on them, and finally devising goals and acting on a plan to achieve them. The nature of the problem is not defined, and could be from any domain of the patient's life – social, emotional or practical, to name a few. Neither does the model define the solution. It does, however, suggest ways in which to accurately identify both the problems and possible solutions.

There are very often a series of sub-problems faced by people living with cancer – being tired, difficulties eating, in general having to rearrange life to accommodate the uncertainty and change that cancer brings. The solutions to these are only partly medical, and often rely on active participation of the patient to implement the plan designed to overcome the problem. If the health professional acknowledges the active role and responsibility of the patient then the relationship between the two can be used as an vehicle to help the patient develop their own resources to tackle the problem. A common example is that of the patient's involvement in treatment decision making.

> Jane was a 73-year-old woman with a diagnosis of advanced pancreatic cancer. She had received initial treatment for her disease, but had experienced a relapse. She was offered the option of further chemotherapy and sought help when conflict arose between herself and her family. Jane's biggest priority was to maintain her quality of life, and while she was somewhat fatigued she was able to undertake most of her daily activities. She was aware that refusing the chemotherapy was likely to mean a shorter life expectancy, but the debilitating side effects she experienced during her previous treatment made her inclined to refuse it. She had raised this with her family, who had become very distressed and tried to convince her to accept the treatment. Jane was able to discuss the issues with her GP, who helped her explore the decision to refuse chemotherapy and to plan how to deal with her family's distress.

We will now explore the three stages of the process in order: exploration, new perspectives and action.

Stage one: exploration

The aim of this stage is to elicit and explore the relevant presenting problems from the point of view of the patient – allowing them to tell the story. Anything that may have a bearing on the patient's adjustment to cancer could be considered relevant. Helping the patient to do this involves recognizing when they are flagging up a concern, asking questions when those cues arise and seeking clarification if anything is unclear. Crucially, patients need to be given time to explain the situation in order to disclose all that is relevant as they may initially disclose less important concerns in order to test the reaction of the health professional concerned. The patient may then follow these with the difficulty that is most pressing, once the health professional's performance has been appraised. Sometimes after identifying one problem, the patient and the health professional immediately get caught up in what to do about it and so miss other important issues. It is therefore important to be systematic in exploring all the concerns of the patient before acting upon them.

A common focus for discussion is the meaning of someone's disease and it is always important to explore this. With any patient you can explore what they think is wrong and the symptoms it is causing, as well as the course they believe it will take, whether it can be controlled, and what they believe the consequences to be. You might also explore what has influenced the particular meaning the patient has given it, bearing in mind that they might be repeating what they have been told rather than what they really believe to be the case.

Although problems specifically related to the disease are important, the patient may also be experiencing more general problems. Any number of other difficulties, such as concerns about children, work or spouse, can potentially impact upon psychological well-being and how someone responds to cancer.

> John, a self-employed accountant in his early thirties, was diagnosed with testicular cancer. His initial response was to become extremely concerned about his financial situation, as he had no idea how he would support himself and his family if he was unable to work. This area would require exploration as it clearly was an important problem.

As well as getting a picture of the problems themselves, this stage should also include eliciting how the patient appraises each of them. This might include whether they believe it to be under their control, or perhaps that someone else is seen as responsible for remedying the situation. Finally, there is also the patient's emotional reaction to each problem: are they feeling anxiety, or perhaps hopelessness in the face of what is seen as an insurmountable problem?

At the point of initial diagnosis, this will include the patient's appraisal of the disease itself. As discussed in chapter 3, patients vary in their beliefs, for example about the possibility of curing cancer and the steps required to achieve cure. Some put their faith in conventional medicine, whereas others seek assistance from alternative practitioners or believe that adopting a particular dietary habit offers hope.

Perhaps at this time, more than any other, it is essential for the health professionals to be aware of their own biases. The way we think, what we attend to and remember, can have a significant effect on which of the patient's cues we respond to. Professionals' concerns about being able to manage patients' distress associated with death, for example, can lead to blocking those cues.

> Elizabeth was a very fearful woman with a straightforward melanoma (skin cancer) that, in her oncologist's opinion, should give very little cause for alarm. Having seen and heard a great deal of publicity about the potentially fatal consequences of developing a melanoma, Elizabeth had become very distressed. Her oncologist's knowledge that her prognosis was good made it hard for him to recognize Elizabeth's distress at first, offering reassurance rather than exploring her perceptions of the situation.

Clarifying problems in a systematic way can have an immediate impact on a patient, giving the sense of 'knowing what I'm up against'.

> Patricia was a young, recently married woman in her mid-thirties. She had a successful career in the civil service, but had recently been diagnosed with breast cancer treated with a lumpectomy. Patricia had been offered additional chemotherapy. She made an appointment to discuss the chemotherapy with her general practitioner because she was unsure about proceeding. During the discussion it become clear that although Patricia was nervous about the possible short-term side effects of the chemotherapy, she was more concerned about the possible effect on her fertility. She was terrified that it would prevent her having children and possibly damage her relationship with her husband.

The identification of Patricia's problem is not the end of the story, however, and the next stage is developing new perspectives.

Stage two: new perspectives

The aim of the second stage of the helping process is to help the patient form a helpful new perspective on the problem you have been exploring with them.

We all have our own habits regarding how we see the obstacles that we encounter, and this can limit us in our ability to overcome them. Trying to find a different way of looking at the problem is helpful as a way of opening up new possible ways forward. It is not the end in itself, but a stepping stone towards dealing effectively with the problem experienced.

The health professional's role is to facilitate the formation of a revised view of the situation, which may in part have been achieved by the systematic exploration of the problem which has gone before. Given the importance of how our understanding of situations guides our reactions to them, this is often a critical stage. Simply providing people with adequate information is a key way in which to assist with this process. Patricia's situation, which we discussed in the last section, is a good example of this. She and her husband were keen to have children, but she had feared this would not happen if she accepted the chemotherapy that had been suggested.

Patricia and her general practitioner discussed the problem at length, and were able to identify that she believed that there was a 100 per cent chance that she would become completely infertile as a result of the treatment, and that there was nothing that could be done to help her. Her GP was able to provide her with an explanation of the probability of specific fertility difficulties associated with the treatment, and to provide her with written information and a referral to an information service. Secondly, the GP discussed with her some of the options that might be available to her if her fertility should be compromised by the chemotherapy. Finally, Patricia agreed to read some information provided by her general practitioner and return with her husband in a week to discuss their reactions to it. When she left the surgery, Patricia reported feeling more hopeful about the situation and keen to find out more about the ideas her GP had raised.

Stage three: action

This final stage aims to move the patient towards a way of managing their problem.

There are a number of steps to follow through, the first of which involves identifying goals.

Setting goals This involves achieving a clear view of what you are both working towards. Goals are a statement of the end point you would like to reach. An example might be making a decision about which treatment option to pursue. Goals help to focus those involved on what needs to be done, provide motivation when a course of action is proving difficult and offer a yardstick against which to evaluate progress. In the context of the helping relationship it can ensure a shared understanding and clear expectations.

Very often the patient's goals are never discussed with the health professional, and when they are there is a tendency for them to be vague. Such vagueness can sometimes cause confusion, however, as the lack of clarity presents an opportunity for misunderstanding. This can also then lead to conflict and resentment when the patient feels let down that the goal is not achieved.

> Enid identified with Julie, her practice nurse, that she wanted to 'get back to normal' after completing treatment for early-stage breast cancer. Julie helped her to be more specific about what being back to normal would include, and they identified a range of activities that she had ceased during treatment and set some goals for returning to them. Enid prioritized visiting her elderly mother once a week for an hour and playing with her grandchild twice a week at her daughter's home as the first goals she wanted to achieve.

Effective goal setting involves deciding a specific, measurable outcome, which is realistic and attainable, and the time-scale in which it is to be achieved. A patient who is unsure about which treatment option to pursue might thus set the goal of deciding whether to accept treatment X or treatment Y by the next appointment with the doctor. An additional crucial element is that the goals set are owned by the patient, so that they value and feel committed to them.

In the context of the helping relationship it is important to come to mutually agreeable goals. This is not always an easy task as the patient may want something that is not, in the view of the health professional, attainable or realistic. For example, during the initial period after it became possible to identify women at risk of breast cancer because they are carrying the BRCA1 gene, there were a number of reports in the media about women who wanted prophylactic mastectomies (that is removal of breast tissue prior to the development of the disease). This goal was seen by some as unreasonable, whereas others took the view that it was a realistic response to the threat of getting breast cancer. Differences in opinion between the patient and the professional have the potential to undermine the working relationship if not handled sensitively.

While some problems are simply tackled, others are more complex and may involve a series of steps with a new goal for each step. At each stage the progress towards the final, or superordinate, goal may need to be reviewed, and at times it will need to be adjusted.

Planning and taking action These are the final steps and involve developing, implementing and evaluating the plans that might be used to achieve the goals that have been set. Such plans must initially be generated, and this is perhaps best done through the process of brainstorming. Brainstorming involves thinking of as many strategies as possible without ruling any out. Only when all the possibilities have been explored are they evaluated in terms of the contribution each could make towards achieving the goals and the practicalities of using each strategy.

People are inclined to repetitively use the same set of problem-solving strategies, regardless of the problem faced. The brainstorming stage is important as a way of preventing this. The health professionals then act as supporters and encouragers for patients while the plans are put into action. They can also provide a sounding-board for patients, helping them to evaluate the effectiveness of the plan and its implementation.

Like any set of goals that people try to achieve, the first plan and attempt to achieve the goals may not work out as hoped. Strategies may not be effective or they may not be practical to implement. Reviewing the relevant goals, and revising the plan accordingly is an integral part of this approach. A good example is when curative treatment is not working, and continued treatment with that goal in mind is not appropriate. This is a stressful time for both the patient and the professionals involved. What is needed is an honest discussion about the goal of cure being no longer realistic, but this may be avoided for fear of distress to either party.

In Patricia's situation, she and her general practitioner identified a number of sources of information relating to the goals she had set herself. These included her clinical oncologist, with whom she made an appointment to discuss the problem, and a local information and support service for people with cancer, where she discussed practical options, such as harvesting and storage of ova and adoption. Patricia's problems as a result of having cancer were not entirely resolved by this process. However, she reported to her general practitioner when she returned to see him that she felt more in control of the situation; she felt as if choices were available to her, when before the situation had seemed black and white. This was not the end of the process for Patricia, as she went on to monitor her progress towards her goal of having children, reviewing whether the strategies she had chosen to use were successful and seeking further assistance as required.

As with all plans, reviewing how its implementation has contributed to the goal being achieved is important but often overlooked. If the plan was not successful further progress can be made by examining why and revising the plan accordingly. If the plan was incompletely or incorrectly implemented a further attempt to carry it out might be helpful. If the plan was successful, reviewing why this was the case can help the patient feel more confident about tackling any future difficulties.

Conclusions

In this chapter we have tried to describe both the nature of the helping relationship and the process of helping. There has been a significant change in recent decades in how we characterize effective relationships between professionals and patients. In contemporary health care the patient is seen as an active partner, with professionals acting as consultants. The relationship between them is one in which the professional assists the patient towards greater well-being through tackling the obstacles and problems identified.

A range of factors are thought to affect the nature of the helping relationship: the setting, health professional factors and patient factors. Factors from each domain interact to facilitate or impede progress. Particular attention has been focused on the beliefs of both professionals and patients as they are so influential in shaping their emotional and behavioural reactions to situations. The process of helping itself can be thought of in stages: initially exploring the problems, secondly developing a new perspective on them, and finally taking action on the goals set by developing, implementing and evaluating plans.

This approach does not dictate what the problem is; that is for the health professional and the patient to define, but may include needing information, practical assistance or support to deal with the emotional consequences of cancer. Equally, we are not assuming which of the possible ways of tackling the problems will be selected or be successful – these will be different for different problems. However, we have reviewed some of the fundamental building blocks of the helping relationship, which include empathy, respect and genuineness, and the ways in which helping relationship can be affected by a wide range of factors. Awareness of these will improve the quality of communication in any situation. The brief outline of the process of helping at the end of this chapter will be expanded throughout the rest of the book. We will be looking at the skills involved in developing and sustaining the helping relationship and how to use the helping process to assist patients with their problems. We will also look at using these strategies to manage routine tasks of communication in cancer care, such as breaking bad news.

Summary

- The relationship between health professionals and their patients is now one of equal partnership, known as the helping relationship.
- This relationship is important as it helps services to meet the basic needs of the patient in receiving good-quality information about their condition and its management, as well as helping them to play an active part in the decision-making process as it relates to their care.
- In addition, it can improve the patient's well-being when used to help tackle the concerns of an individual patient, and so help them to help themselves in dealing with the everyday challenges associated with having cancer.
- The quality of the helping relationship is affected by the fundamental attitude taken by the health professional towards his or her patient. At best this involves having an empathic understanding of the patient's concerns, showing respect towards the patient and being genuine in one's work as a health professional.
- Other factors which affect the relationship include those relating to the setting in which the health professional and patient meet, and the beliefs, emotions and behaviours of the health professional and the patient equally. These can interact with one another to either enhance or undermine the relationship.
- The process of helping patients includes identifying problems, gaining new perspectives and taking action by setting goals then generating problem-solving strategies that are reviewed and amended as appropriate.
- This process can be used with any problem identified by a patient, and it does not assume either the nature of the problem or the solution.

Chapter Five

The Building-Blocks of Communication

In this chapter we will be focusing on the communication and counselling skills that you can use to implement the helping process. Good communication results from the use of a set of skills that can be taught and learned, and practice can improve the skills over time. Although there are many core communication skills, they are used somewhat differently in the various stages of the helping process that we described in the last chapter.

The skills can be thought of as forming a pyramid:

- stage 1 – exploration: the bedrock is paying close attention to the patient and clarifying the situation through active listening;
- stage 2 – new perspectives: joining the patient in trying to make sense of the situation through exploring the situation further and beginning to consider options for change forms the second layer;
- stage 3 – action: deciding on goals and making and implementing a plan of action is the pinnacle.

Each layer of skills builds upon the previous layers; hence it is preferable to learn about them in that order, as we will do now.

Stage 1: Exploration

Perhaps the single most valuable set of skills to learn in communication are those of active listening – they are used at all stages of the helping process and underpin the skills used in later stages. Once acquired they stand you in good stead to tackle most of the clinical situations you will face. Active listening skills are the basic tools you can use to understand how the patient makes sense of the situation, or to empathize with them and pick up cues about issues that are of concern to them. They are also used to communicate that understanding and acceptance to the patient. The first step is to show that you are listening.

Show that you are listening

Communication is often thought of as speech. However, listening is perhaps more important still. At the most basic level a good relationship requires that you pay attention to the other person. However, it is also necessary that the patient realizes that this is what you are doing. A few key behaviours serve to show that you are paying attention and are ready to listen:

- face your patient;
- sit in an open and relaxed posture;
- lean slightly towards the patient;
- maintain good eye contact.

When these signs of paying attention are shown, the patient is more likely to continue to discuss the situation with you.

Brief verbal and non-verbal communications, known as minimal encouragers, can also be used to show that you are paying attention. These minimal encouragers include nodding or quietly making comments, such as 'yes' or 'I see'. Even these very small behavioural responses add to the evidence for the patient that you are interested in what is being said and are paying attention.

You should bear in mind that these rules of thumb may be applicable only to the majority of American and British patients. Modifications may be required to ensure that your behaviour means the same to someone from a different culture. Eye contact can be seen as confrontational in some cultures, for example. Make use of the resources provided by local interpretation services or others, for guidance. If your patients do not speak English as a first language it may be appropriate to employ an interpreter.

Observe your patient closely

There are a number of important aspects of your patient's presentation that you can observe as part of your strategy to listen actively: (i) emotional content; (ii) non-verbal behaviours; and (iii) patterns of behaviour.

Listen to the emotional content Paying close attention to the details of both the factual content (the story) and the emotional content (how the patient feels about it) of what is said is vital. Many clinical situations involve listening, but very often the listener misses important elements of what the speaker is saying by concentrating only on the factual content. It is equally important to listen for clues about how events have impacted emotionally, as well as about the strengths that the patient has in facing the situation. The specific choice of words to describe events offers rich clues in this respect. This is very clear in patients' descriptions of pain, which may vary from 'ache', through more distressing adjectives such as 'annoying' or even 'sickening'. They may also give verbal clues to the model of the situation that has been formed, as in the example below.

Compare the following brief excerpts from two different patients relating their experiences of being told they had cancer. The first patient reported: 'Mr X was very kind, he discussed the whole thing with me and let me interrupt and ask questions as we went through.' The second patient had a different experience, and reported: 'He gave me the news, just like that, and told me to come back the next week for further tests.' At face value they are both describing the facts of the bad news interview, but they are also communicating how they felt about it. Clearly the use of words like 'kind' in the first report and 'told me' in the second convey important information about how they felt they were being treated. The second patient mentioned that 'there was no choice, that was that', reflecting his view that the future was in someone else's hands and out of his control. Such observations reveal important facets of the presenting problem.

Non-verbal clues As well as listening to the patient's words, we can also attend to non-verbal clues. Patients who sigh frequently or fail to make eye contact with you are providing clues about how they feel in general, and specifically about the particular topic being discussed. Equally a patient with clenched fists might be leaking a feeling of anger, and another who is reluctant to sit and would rather pace around the room may be displaying a sign of anxiety.

Observe patterns of behaviour Throughout the interview listen out for all the ways in which the patient is trying to communicate and take note of how they fit together into patterns. Equally make observations about discrepancies in the presentation, for example a smiling patient whose speech is slow or monotone. Such signs may help you to identify people with mood changes, such as depression as described in chapter 3. Avoidance, or in other cases the repetition, of a particular theme offers clues about how the patient sees the situation and those issues that may be worrying or challenging.

A GP discussing an urgent referral to hospital for a gentleman with worrying symptoms indicative of lung cancer mentioned numerous times to his patient that he was concerned about the symptoms. He called them 'serious' and 'worrying', and gave his patient every hint that he had a strong suspicion that they suggested that the cause of the symptoms was cancer. However, his patient seemed to glide over all the references and remained cheerful throughout. He checked with the GP at the end of the consultation that it was really necessary to go to hospital, saying 'couldn't you just give me one of those inhaler thingies' that he had seen his daughter use to control her asthma. These observations provide clues to the problem as the patient sees it. It can also help to alert you to areas for further exploration as you move into clarifying and exploring the problem in more depth.

Reflection, summarizing and paraphrasing

Reflection involves feeding back to the patient what you have heard them say (content) or how they seem to be feeling (emotion). It is one of the simplest of the active listening strategies.

You can reflect the content, or narrative, by repeating words that have been used by your patient, most easily those at end of the sentence, to show that you have listened and understood. Try to avoid sounding like a parrot, however – overuse of reflection diminishes its effectiveness and you run the risk of sounding patronizing.

It is not only the facts of the story being told that can be reflected. More sophisticated forms include reflecting back the emotions conveyed, for example:

> *'You're sounding pretty hopeless about the whole thing',*
> *'So you've concentrated on finding out more and talking to Sally about it?'*

Routinely reflecting the emotional content helps to give the message that you find it an acceptable area to discuss. This can increase your patient's confidence in raising difficult emotional issues with you at a later stage of the interview or relationship.

Jenny went to see her GP after receiving a diagnosis of breast cancer and being offered the option of either mastectomy or lumpectomy and local radiotherapy. In this excerpt Jenny has already explained the facts of the situation to her GP, and is now going on to describe her reaction to it.

> *Jenny:* I just don't know what to do for the best, it's such a confusing situation and on top of everything else that has happened I sometimes think I just can't cope with this too.
>
> *GP:* You say you don't think that you can cope with this too? *(reflection)*
>
> *Jenny:* Yes, I really thought that I had overcome most things that life could throw at me. I mean I had a dreadful time as a child, but I pulled myself through it and then met Ron, which was great. Of course, we both desperately wanted children and when we found out we couldn't I got depressed, but I consoled myself by thinking that I must have had my share of problems then. But then he was killed, and I guess I thought after three years I was just getting my life together again then this happened. It just seems so unfair.

The GP in this situation picks up on Jenny's statement that she could not cope. Reflecting this back to her elicited a rich account of her feeling of being under siege from difficulties and unable to cope. It also served to indicate his interest and understanding of her situation.

When patients give a lengthy description or account, a summary statement can be used. Summaries draw together the main concepts being expressed. They can act as full stops in the discussion when large chunks of information are fed back to the patient, allowing them an opportunity to correct or elaborate as necessary. They are also an effective way of moving the patient on to the next topic to explore when followed by a cue to do so, for example: 'So the weight gain is a big concern. Does anything else concern you?'

There is an important note of caution to be sounded in the use of reflection and summaries. If overused patients can find them irritating as they may seem rather mechanical. This can be avoided by paraphrasing what the patient has said or using common expressions or phrases to sum up. The use of metaphors and analogies, such as 'like the weight being lifted off your shoulders' or 'being in a deep pit' can equally well convey a strong sense of the emotional reaction of the patient.

Open questions

These are questions that are designed to help patients explore their situation. This can include explaining their thoughts and telling you more about their perception of how different factors influence each other. They often start with words like 'what', 'how' or 'why', such as 'What do you think is causing the nausea you have been experiencing?' By contrast, closed questions, such as 'Do you think it's the chemotherapy causing the sickness?', are a reflection of the health professional's agenda and can generally only be answered with a yes or no. The latter has the effect of preventing disclosure of concerns and may mean you have lost an opportunity to find out more. However, at times you may wish to use closed questions to clarify the presence or absence of a particular symptom that is important to diagnosis or management.

Open questions can be useful to help understand some of the events that trigger off particular problems, and the consequences of them. Where difficulties are intermittent, exploring the situations in which they occur, what triggers them and how patients attempt to deal with them can offer useful insights about the nature of the problem as a whole.

This can be done with a series of open questions:

'Under what circumstances do you experience the problem?'
'What happens afterwards?'
'What do you do to try to manage the situation, and does it help?'

Focusing

At times you may want your patient to elaborate on a particular issue and this can be achieved by use of reflection techniques and specific questions. In line with our previous review of the importance of thoughts, feelings and behaviours, you may want to focus on any changes in the domains that accompany the reported problem, for example by asking at those times:

'What feelings do you experience?'
'What goes through your mind?'
'Do you notice any changes in your body, for example butterflies or changes to your breathing?'

All of the skills involved in paying careful attention and listening actively, when used together, allow you to explore the presenting problem with the patient. The following excerpt illustrates the use of some of these techniques when a patient, John, attends his first appointment with his GP after being discharged from hospital following surgery for stomach cancer. In this case, the GP is using all of the basic active listening strategies that we have explored in the section so far, and they are marked in the text.

> *GP:* So, John, it's a while since we last met and I received a letter from the hospital earlier this week saying that you had been discharged after your operation. Could you help me understand what has been happening since we last met?
>
> *John:* Well, I saw the doc at the hospital and he said I had to go in straight

away and have the op done. (sighs)

GP: So, you saw him and were admitted, yeah? (*reflection*)

John: I had the op the next day . . . (pauses and looks down)

GP: The next day. (*reflection*) (nods) (*minimal encourager*)

John: (sighs and pauses) I felt terrible, so sick and in pain, and I was thinking this must be a bad sign, to feel so bad and be admitted so quickly.

GP: So you went in and had the op quite quickly and afterwards felt terrible, which in itself worried you. (*summarizing*) It sounds as though it was a difficult time, and it's still difficult to talk about now. (*reflection of emotional content*)

John: It certainly was. I try not to think about it now I'm home.

In this scenario the GP has listened to both the factual and emotional content of what John has said to him and used reflection and minimal encouragers to help him to tell his story. Finally, he has drawn together the general message of what John said in a summary paragraph providing an opportunity to move the interview on in any appropriate direction at that point. The GP has also demonstrated his empathy for John's situation – he has fed back to him both what happened and how he felt about it. John's response to this suggests that the summary was on target, and he has given his GP further information by telling him he now tries to avoid thinking about it. The GP has now established the basic outline of the presenting problem as experienced by the patient, and is ready to move on to exploring it in more detail.

These skills are vital to allow you to form a broad understanding of how your patient makes sense of the situation. Their use is equally crucial to your patient, who is more likely to feel understood by you as a result. Encouraging your patient to examine the situation systematically may start the process of thinking about it differently. The assessment in itself becomes therapeutic and opens the door to the next stage in the helping process. All of these skills are also used in the later stages of the helping process, albeit to achieve slightly different aims. Mastering them is therefore extremely important and ultimately this can only be achieved by practice.

✳ *Developing your skills*

- You can improve your ability to pay attention to the various ways in which people communicate by practising in everyday situations. Even standing at a bus stop can provide an opportunity to study the body language of those around you, or listen to the emotional tone of conversations to sharpen up your skills.

- Tape-recording your interviews with patients is an excellent way to develop a better awareness of how you are already communicating. You might like to try to analyse whether you are already using any of the skills, or similar strategies to help your patients explore their problems. You can also look out for missed opportunities – perhaps a time when you have used a closed rather than an open question or missed picking up a cue from a patient that there is something important on their mind. If you do choose this strategy to help you improve your communication skills, then check out local arrangements for seeking consent and storage and destruction of recordings. Given the frequent concerns raised by patients about health professionals' communication skills, you may find that they are more than happy to help you improve yours!

- Others around you may also be prepared to give you feedback about your performance. If you identify a particular skill you want to work on, then why not try it out in casual conversations and hone your skills that way?

Stage 2: New Perspectives

Helping a person to explore and clarify their concerns often facilitates a reappraisal of their situation; it can also help them to identify ways in which they may be able to adapt to it. Change, however, is something that people often resist, although we frequently engage in an ongoing search for understanding of our circumstances, as we discussed in chapter 3. At times, however, a patient may reached an impasse with a problem and struggle to make progress.

At this stage, health professionals turn from understanding and clarifying the patient's view of the situation, to helping the patient form a revised, more helpful model of their situation and their responses to it, both internal (thoughts and feelings) and external (behaviour). A new perspective is not the end point, however, but is intended to be a launching pad for action, the skills for which are examined in the final sections of this chapter.

The skills that are required include all of those discussed in the previous sections of the chapter. However, there are some additional ones that can be particularly helpful at this stage. These are often referred to as challenging skills (Egan 1998) and comprise three main elements:

- providing information to help the patient form a more accurate or adaptive model of the situation, such as the number of patients experiencing nausea and vomiting with particular chemotherapy regimes;
- helping patients understand more fully how they see the situation by

sharing your hunches about it (known as advanced empathy), for example suggesting that what may be stopping them from adhering to a pain medication regime that could help control their pain could be an unhelpful underlying belief that they will become addicted to pain-killers;

- challenging patients' unhelpful thoughts and beliefs about the situation and their responses. For example, these might include a belief that only health professionals have the power to do anything about a patient's health problem, so that they do not try out any self-help strategies. This is best challenged by encouraging patients themselves to weigh up the utility of looking at the situation in a particular way and consciously developing a new way to look at it that is more helpful.

Providing information

The routine provision of information often acts as a prompt to rethink the situation in a new light. We will be describing how to do this effectively as a part of your routine practice in more detail in the next chapter, including some guidelines for best practice.

Inquiring about the patient's level of understanding allows you to assess the situation more effectively, perhaps by asking:

'Could you tell me what you understand about the situation so far?'

This provides you with an opportunity to pinpoint exactly what information may be required, and you can then provide it. In the event that you suspect that the patient is lacking important information or has misunderstood something, you may wish to provide some specific information. Checking out with the patient how they have formed the view they have can enable you to identify any points of misinformation. You can ask what the patient is basing their view on: 'What has led you to think that?' When patients report that another health professional has given them particular information, it can be important to check out how they have interpreted that information: 'What did you understand them to mean?'

It is important to note here the fragility of new perspectives. When the patient leaves a consultation with a new view of something, they need some time to assimilate the new information. Backing up verbal information with written material can help them remember what has been discussed. This can take the form of carefully selected leaflets, or a copy of the summary letter sent to another professional or even a tape of the interview. There is further advice about this in the next chapter.

At times you may not be able to provide the information required by your patient, but can help them to form a strategy to obtain the information they need. This can include preparing for consultations with other health professionals by compiling a list of questions, or acting as a conduit by recommending other reliable sources of advice, for example some of the cancer charities who provide information direct to patients.

Another source of information is the self. Monitoring one's own behaviour is an excellent way of testing out the assumptions we make about situations. The new information may then challenge the pre-existing model that the patient had formed. Recording the occurrence of a problem in a diary can provide useful information about some of the factors that might influence it. This may include:

- triggers, that is things that set off a problem, such as overdoing an activity and thereby exacerbating pain;
- maintaining factors, that is, things that keep a problem going, such as brief relief following reassurance by a doctor which inclines the patient to seek further reassurance during future periods of anxiety or doubt.

Encourage the patient to make a note of the situation in which the problem occurred, what else was happening at the time, including thoughts and feelings, and what happened as a result. The diary can then be used during a meeting to look at how different events impact upon each other. It can serve to test out some of the predictions and assumptions about important triggers or maintaining factors and a revised model of the problem can then be developed.

This method was used to help Rita, who was receiving chemotherapy for lung cancer and became very distressed during periods of breathlessness. She had spoken with her nurse, John, saying that she thought the chemotherapy was not working and her disease was progressing. Alongside standard medical investigations about her concerns, she kept a diary of when the periods of breathlessness occurred, and how she responded to them. After a week of recording, it became clear that they were more likely to happen when she was expecting visitors. During these times she found herself thinking that they would be shocked to see the house untidy, and she would push herself to try to tidy up. She would then start to feel breathless, and would become anxious that it was a sign of her disease progressing. John was then able to help her form a new perspective about her symptoms based on the information she herself had collected.

John: So, Rita, how did you get along with the diary you were keeping of the breathlessness you were experiencing?

Rita: Well, I did as you asked, but I'm not sure what to make of it – it seems to happen more in the afternoons from what I can see. (gets out the diary and hands it to John)

John: Let's have a look together, shall we? So it happened on four of the days since we last met eight days ago, is that right? (*summary*) (Rita nods) And it seemed to happen more in the afternoon, but this one here happened in the morning, is that right? (*checking out*)

Rita: Yes, that's right.

John: Is there anything else that is common to these situations, do you think? (*open question*)

Rita: Well they were all busy times, I remember, I was getting ready for someone to visit.

John: What were you doing during those times, when you were waiting for visitors to arrive? (*open question*)

Rita: Well, I was thinking what a state the place is and I really ought to tidy up. They'd be shocked to see it in such a mess, I'd try to sort it out a bit, make it respectable, you know.

John: Well, I wonder, Rita, whether that might have something to do with the breathlessness you had. As we discussed last time, there's no other evidence that things are getting worse with your disease, but you've been very ill and maybe rushing around might be enough to make anyone who has been so ill rather breathless? (*tentative suggestion of new perspective*) What do you think? (*open question*)

Rita: I suppose you might have a point, but I do worry about it.

This discussion demonstrates how the combination of using some of the active listening and exploration techniques we described in the previous sections can be integrated with specific challenging techniques to help patients get a rounder view of the situation. In turn, challenging helps the problem-solving process by implicating a wider range of targets for intervention.

Rita now has an alternative explanation for her symptoms that is not compatible with solutions involving changing her treatment or giving up hope of controlling her disease. Now she may consider strategies based on the competing hypothesis, such as reducing her expectations of herself in keeping her home as tidy as she did previously, or changing how she tackles the task of tidying up so that it does not result in overdoing her activity level and bringing on the symptoms of breathlessness.

Advanced empathy

At this stage it can be helpful to look beneath the surface level and highlight unspoken ideas. The benefit for your patient is gained from your reporting to them these hunches about what may lie under the surface. There are a number of different sorts of hunches that we will now explore in detail: making the implicit explicit, identifying themes and reality checking.

Making the implicit explicit if your patient appears to be operating on a particular belief, but has not stated it, you may want to point this out. People do not always make explicit the things that concern them most. They may also, at times, be unaware of the influence of some of their underlying beliefs on their response to the situation. It can be possible to make educated guesses partly in response to how you feel when talking with the patient. If you find yourself feeling increasingly hopeless or anxious about the situation you may want to explore whether this feeling is shared by the patient. Feeding back such hunches to the patient can help to bring the patient's feelings into relief, but also underline your empathy for them.

> '*I wonder if this makes you feel pretty lonely and vulnerable now the treatment is finished and you are home alone during the day?*'

This may lead the patient to understand their situation differently – a bit like adding the final piece of a jigsaw that makes all the other pieces make sense as a whole.

Identifying themes Drawing together and pointing out common themes that appear to play a part in apparently unrelated issues may also be useful. As an observer you may find it easier to spot some of the patterns that your patient describes in a number of different situations. Sometimes these themes can be linked with past events, but they may solely relate to aspects of the patient's cancer experience. A pertinent theme for people with cancer may be the sense that, in retrospect, early signs or symptoms from a cancer were missed.

> '*It seems to me that this is not the first time that you have felt out of control. I know you haven't spoken about it much, but you mentioned that you also felt that way during your marriage and at school – in those situations you felt there was no option but to wait for other people to rescue you too? Do you think there is any similarity with how you are thinking and feeling now?*'

When disparate parts of a problem are linked together in this way, it can help the situation seem more manageable, as there is only one, rather than multiple problems to be faced. Again reflection and open questions are extremely useful tools in encouraging the patient to reconsider all the pieces of the jigsaw.

In this situation a GP is discussing with his patient Jenny, who we first heard about earlier in the chapter, her difficulties sleeping. He had previously helped to support her when her husband, Ron, had died unexpectedly. The following shows how Jenny's GP carefully explores the situation with her, and then challenges her by sharing his hunch:

> *GP:* It sounds as though the sense that you can't cope is very strong at times. When are those feelings worse? (*open question*)
> *Jenny:* Well, it's there most of the time, but it's worse at night.
> *GP:* Did you get that feeling last night? (*clarifying through closed question*)
> *Jenny:* Yes, I did. I couldn't get to sleep and I was just feeling so desperate, thinking about the radiotherapy and having to go to the hospital every day for all those weeks.
> *GP:* So last night you were feeling as though you couldn't cope and thinking about the travel that the radiotherapy would involve. (*summary*) What were you thinking about the radiotherapy? (*open question*)
> *Jenny:* I feel so dreadful, and I just can't imagine getting myself up and ready, and to the hospital every day for all that time. I just couldn't cope with the travelling, and I couldn't afford it anyway. But I don't want to lose my breast – who would ever want me then?
> *GP:* I wonder whether this might be reminding you of how you felt when Ron died? (*making the implicit explicit and identifying a theme*)

The GP helped to draw out of Jenny the course of events that led up to her feeling of not being able to cope. He also helps her to see that the feeling itself triggers off yet more emotional memories, and reminders of difficult times in her past which compound her distress. This is a theme that could be highlighted for her if she did not spontaneously identify it herself. This more detailed understanding of the situation offers opportunities for the two to evaluate her thoughts about the challenges that face her, as well as suggesting some possible points for intervention, for example dealing with her late-night tendency to worry.

Reality checking The messages from patients can sometimes contradict each other. For example, what a patient does and says may not match each other, or there may be apparent inconsistencies in the patient's model of the situation. Health professionals can share hunches with the patient that there may be more to the situation than meets the eye by feeding back these inconsistencies. You can then make good use of reflection and questioning skills to explore such contradictions and encourage the patient to reappraise the situation. This can include reflecting the contrast between someone's body language and what is being said, such as a patient making no eye contact and sitting slumped in a chair, but saying that they are feeling fine.

It may also be appropriate to highlight a patient's view that they are not coping if it appears to be inconsistent with the facts. Patients commonly find it difficult to adjust their expectations of themselves, and so regard themselves as failing if they do not achieve all that they normally would. Normalizing common experiences of anger, distress, pain or fatigue can help patients to see themselves as ordinary in their reactions to cancer, rather than abnormal.

'I find it hard to accept that you really are fine, when everything about how you are behaving today says otherwise – I'm not sure that you have smiled even once. What do you think is going on?'

Helping the patient to explore such mismatches may lead to a revision of their understanding of the situation and highlight possible areas for change.

Challenging unhelpful thoughts and assumptions

At times a direct approach is best to enable the person to review their appraisal of the situation and how it can be managed. If you are planning to take this approach, it is essential that you explain to the patient the idea behind the approach: that we each try to make sense of the situations we find ourselves in but that the understanding we come to is not always the most valid, nor is it always the one that is most helpful to us. You can then invite your patient to join you in assessing the validity of the understanding they have come to about their situation.

The first step is to help the patient identify the assumptions they are making about their situation. Many of those assumptions will have come to light during the exploration of the problem, through the use of open questions about your patient's behaviour, thoughts, emotions and physical sensations as we described above. You can draw on those directly by reminding the patient of them, using summarizing skills to draw together the links between the relevant dimensions, for example:

'I recall that you described yourself thinking "I'm done for" and feeling hopeless when you heard that you had cancer.'

The next step is to identify any assumptions that may need to be tackled. These may include those that are invalid or unhelpful in that they increase distress or undermine personal resources to manage. Inaccurate assumptions, such as overestimating the chances of a cancer being fatal, may result from lack or misunderstanding of information. Assumptions that undermine personal resources may diminish confidence in tackling a problem, for example thinking that there is nothing that will make a difference to it, or increase distress, such as focusing on the 25 per cent chance of dying as a result of a cancer rather than on the rather better odds of surviving.

When actually challenging assumptions, you can assess whether an assumption is accurate or valid by checking out what it is based upon. Simply asking

'*What do you base that on?*' or
'*What's the evidence for assuming that?*'

is sufficient to elicit and examine a person's beliefs. Dealing with thoughts and assumptions that undermine personal resources can be done in two different ways. Firstly, by asking the patient to think through and evaluate the effect on them of thinking of the situation in that way. A patient who is experiencing difficulties sleeping might be asked to consider whether thinking 'go to sleep or suffer tomorrow' is likely to help or hinder them in achieving the goal of getting off to sleep. Secondly, you might just ask:

'*Is it helping you to cope with this to think about it in this way?*'

Encouraging patients to assess the helpfulness of particular thoughts and assumptions is important because it can lead them to develop a more constructive way of thinking about problems and generate alternative solutions.

'*Is there another way that we might think about it that would be more helpful?*'

The following example shows a clinical nurse specialist (CNS) talking through with her patient some concerns about attending for breast screening following previous treatment for breast cancer.

CNS: So Linda, thanks for coming in to see me. You were saying on the telephone that you weren't sure whether to attend for your mammogram. (*summary*) What are you thinking that was leading you to feel that way? (*open question*)

Linda: I'm just so sure that it will pick something up and I'll get caught up in all the treatment again and it would probably kill me this time.

CNS: I can quite understand why you would be reluctant to come for the test with all of those thoughts going through your mind. (*empathy*) You might remember we talked before about the way we all try to make sense of our situation, but we don't always come up with the most helpful way of looking at it. Do you remember when we discussed that before?

Linda: Yes, when I was trying to decide what to do about the chemotherapy that Dr Randolph suggested.

CNS: Well I wonder whether it would be useful to ask ourselves some of the same questions now that we asked then. For instance, what are you basing your prediction on about what would happen if you had the mammogram? (*assess validity*)

Linda: Well, I don't suppose I really have any reason to think it will turn out that way, I'm just frightened it will.

CNS: OK, so maybe it's the worst that could happen. Do you think that seeing it that way is helping you at all? (*assess helpfulness*)

Linda: Well no, not at all. I'm just getting all wound up and anxious about it, when I just want to get on with life.

CNS: So might there be another, more helpful way to think about having the test done, given that you want to be able to get on with life? (*generate alternatives*)

Linda: I guess even if they did find the cancer had come back it would be there even if I didn't have the test. If I have the test and they do find cancer maybe it would be easier to treat than if I waited until I could feel a lump or something.

CNS: So it sounds as though you are saying that avoiding the test won't help you avoid a recurrence. (*summary*) You never know, the test may be clear and you could feel a bit reassured by that perhaps?

The use of the word 'challenging' is not meant to convey a confrontational approach. Open hostility is seldom a viable strategy in effecting lasting and positive change. Clearly success is more likely in helping relationships that are already well developed and these skills need to be applied with respect, and sensitivity. You may like to consider some of the times when you have had your view of the world challenged and under what circumstances you have accepted it and when you have rejected it. It is a privilege and not a right to be able to dig so deeply into someone else's life and it is important to keep this in mind. Helpful guidelines to bear in mind include:

● **Challenge with respect** Challenging skills should be employed in a respectful and non-threatening way that allows the person to consider and question their views, in collaboration with the helper.

- **Take your time** It is important not to rush into challenging someone about how a situation looks to them. You need to listen properly before you can understand, and if you challenge a patient prematurely you are likely appear judgemental.
- **Be tentative** Check out whether the individual can see that their view of the situation is only one possible interpretation rather than the definitive account. This can help you to assess whether looking for new perspectives is likely to be successful at this stage. This can be achieved by the liberal use of open questions and summaries, and crucially by taking time. Using phrases such as 'It seems to me that perhaps . . . ' or 'I wonder if . . .' can help to convey a sense of joint exploration, rather than of a judgement being handed down. It can be all too easy to tip into appearing to lecture the patient about what they *should* think or feel – the common consequence of which is the patient becoming defensive and less likely to consider alternatives.
- **Act as a facilitator** Finally, recall the nature of the helping relationship. It is one in which you, as the helper, are a facilitator for the patient. In the context of such a relationship the aim is to allow the patient to take control of the situation as much as they can. Challenging should not be used to encourage the patient to change their views purely to be more in accord with your own.

Developing your skills

- Identify points of information that you commonly have to explain and practise explaining them to friends or colleagues without specialized knowledge. Get feedback from others about how you are doing, and keep revising it until you are comfortable with how to address it. You may want to develop some crib notes to refresh yourself with at the time.
- Think through how you could share hunches with patients, and perhaps try them out initially on patients with whom you are confident you have a good relationship before taking on more demanding situations.
- Seek the advice of someone with expertise in counselling techniques to give you some feedback on your use of these new strategies and help you think through how to integrate them into your practice.

The various skills we have discussed in this section are designed to encourage the patient to develop their appraisal of the situation. Deeper insight or a new insight, however, is not the end of the story. The helping process is designed to facilitate action on the part of the patient. It is not unusual for patients to start to identify the options open to them at this stage, and we will now turn our attention to the skills that can be used to help the patient take action.

Stage 3: Action

Once the problem areas have been identified and explored, the next stage is to tackle them. There are a number of stages to the process of taking action: choosing the problem to work on, setting goals, identifying an action plan to achieve the goals, reviewing progress and revising the plan until the goal is achieved. We will explore the skills involved in each stage in the next section.

Prioritizing problems

It is common for there to be a number of problems facing a patient at any given time. In such a situation, deciding which to tackle or in what order to tackle them is the initial task. Commonly there are a number of different problems that are often interrelated.

Mary, a 32-year-old single woman, had recently started dating a new boyfriend. Mary's brain tumour had been kept under control with surgery, chemotherapy and radiotherapy over the previous year, but after a recent recurrence she had been prescribed a further course of chemotherapy. Mary understood that the treatment was not curative and that one of the side effects of the course was that she was likely to lose her hair, which was a great concern to her. Mary returned to her oncologist for the first cycle of chemotherapy, only to say that she did not know whether she wanted to go ahead.

The oncologist took some time to discuss Mary's reasons for her indecision, and her deep distress at the prospect of losing her hair became apparent. She told him about the previous inadequate wig she had received and worn, but said she was worried that her new boyfriend would be put off by seeing her in the wig and so she did not want to start the treatment. Mary's assumption was that there was no other option but to wear the old wig, and rather than do that she was prepared to risk not having the treatment prescribed for her. Mary agreed to delay the chemotherapy for a week in order to explore ways of obtaining a wig that was acceptable to her.

There can, at times, be too many problems to tackle at once. When this happens there are a number of different ways to make the choice between them. It may be both useful and important to prioritize them. The patient's own values can be used to help prioritize problems. Attentive listening at earlier stages may allow you to help at this stage by reflecting observations about the patient's values in life, for example that the children always come first, or that work is a means to an end, not an end in itself. Selecting a problem that is a more significant threat to the patient's values is more likely to engage and motivate.

Patients should also be encouraged to prioritize those problems that they are keen to overcome, rather than those that others may wish them to choose. It is much more likely that patients will be motivated to implement the final action plan if it is personally highly relevant. Getting more exercise, for example, may be important to some people, but not all. This is especially true when the solution lies in a patient's own hands, for example lifestyle changes such as changing diet. Other important considerations include which problem is most pressing or causing most distress.

Suggest to your patient that they make a list of the problems identified and then organize them in order of priority, based on any or all of the above considerations. If a patient is not sure about a particular problem, you might suggest that they draw up a list of the pros and cons (also known as a decisional balance) of leaving it or tackling it. This can be a useful aid to decision making.

Goal setting

The process of establishing what someone wants to achieve is known as goal setting. It is something that we all do in everyday life, though we may not label it as such. It can include planning to buy a house or change job, or more modestly cooking a meal. Our goals in life guide our choices and shape our behaviour, including for example how we spend our time and our money.

In identifying a goal, the question is essentially: what do you want to achieve?

Joe was a 65-year-old man who had suffered from prostate cancer, for which he had received a range of different treatments, but his disease continued to progress. Some weeks prior to his admission with pain, as a result of bony metastases, one of the nurses on the ward had suggested to Joe's wife that he might be referred to a local community palliative-care team. Joe's wife had been quite keen, as she was anxious about how she would manage to continue looking after him, but when she mentioned it to Joe he refused. On a number of subsequent occasions it was raised with him again, but was always met with strong rejection. On one occasion he responded to the suggestion by declaring, 'You're just trying to give up on me.' On the third day of his final admission, after many complaints about problems he was experiencing on the ward, Joe finally admitted to his nurse that he realized he was very unwell and that if he was going to die he wanted it to be at home. All of the staff involved in Joe's care were aware that until that point he had refused to face the fact that his condition was declining and that he was even unwilling to acknowledge the possibility of his death. When he did finally come to terms with the inevitability of his death, Joe was able to articulate what he wanted for himself in what is perhaps the ultimate difficult circumstance.

Using open questions can help patients to identify the main goal, particularly if they encourage projection into the future. There are a number of open questions that can help patients to look forward towards a general goal:

- If this problem were sorted out, how would your life be different?
- If you think about yourself three months from now, how would you like life to be for you?
- If you imagine yourself in six months' time, what would be the most important thing that could have changed for you?
- What would you be doing that you are not doing now?
- What things that are part of your life currently would be gone?

Let us return briefly to Joe's situation.

His nurse, Sue, helped him to clarify his goal by asking him a number of questions. She started with a summary of Joe's various comments about how his current situation was not satisfactory to him:

'It sounds as though with all the difficulties you are having you would rather not be here.'

Sue followed this by asking him a version of an open question intended to help him move on to identifying a goal to work towards:

'What would have to be different for you to feel more satisfied with the situation?'

Joe went on to identify a number of factors that would be important for him, which included being able to have some of his favourite foods, see his garden blooming and watch his favourite programme without being disturbed. He then commented:

'If I'm going to be so unwell, and perhaps die, I guess I want to be at home with my own things.'

The principles of effective goal setting are somewhat similar to those that guide the selection of the problem to work on. It is important that they should be personally relevant and consistent with the patient's personal values. It is much easier to draw up an effective plan if the goal is specific rather than vague, for example 'relying less on pain medication and using self-help strategies instead' is better than 'sorting out my pain'. Equally goals benefit from being realistic, in that the person has the capacity to achieve them and they will successfully impact upon the problem identified.

Roger, who had previously been kept extremely busy with his work as a sports teacher, had been forced to take an extended period of sick leave following the diagnosis of testicular cancer. He was bored and lethargic, unable to find anything that could absorb his attention. His mood was getting low and he was socially isolated without any of his colleagues to talk to during the day. Roger went to see the practice nurse, Rebecca, about a minor unrelated physical symptom, and she reflected back to him that he seemed sad. They discussed the situation for a short while, and he described missing his work and his colleagues there, and generally feeling unfit and tired. Roger identified a long-term goal of returning to work, and identified that getting fitter and either overcoming or managing his fatigue would be necessary in order to be able to achieve the goal. The latter two could be considered the sub-goals, or steps towards achieving the final large goal. However, he concluded that returning to work was not going to be quick, and so he decided to concentrate on the problem of having few enjoyable things to do and little social contact as the target to work on initially. He and Rebecca finally agreed that the goal would be doing something enjoyable and sociable each day, gradually introducing short activities and slowly building up until he was able to do this every day in eight weeks' time.

Planning for action

Once you have decided the goal, or destination, what is needed next is a map, or an effective plan intended to reach that point. People usually have characteristic ways of approaching difficult situations, including what they recognize as a problem, what problems they choose to tackle and how they tackle them. The risk is that they do not always implement the most suitable solution.

It can be important, therefore, to encourage patients to identify those strategies which may be most effective in a specific situation, rather than swinging straight into action. Brainstorming can be a useful strategy at this stage, in that it encourages patients to consider *all* possibilities without ruling anything out. It is intended as a prompt to suspend judgement and shake off the everyday limitations we place upon our thinking – what is proper, what others expect, what we think ourselves capable of – with a view to sorting through them and evaluating them at a later time.

Roger and his nurse, Rebecca, had identified the goal of doing something enjoyable and sociable every day. They decided to try to identify some of the activities that used to give him pleasure to try to find a way of meeting his needs. However, they concluded that all were unsuitable for him at that time, and so Rebecca suggested they try to brainstorm some ideas of enjoyable activities.

Rebecca: Roger, can I suggest that we try a little exercise to see if we can come up with some ways of helping you find some enjoyable activities to occupy you. You may have heard of the idea of brainstorming before – are you familiar with it?

Roger: I certainly am – it's about trying to be creative, isn't it?

Rebecca: That's a good way of thinking about it. It works best if you suspend any tendency to judge the ideas you come up with until such time as you have completely run out of ideas. Then we can go back and weigh them up and see which might fit the bill and which might actually be usable! (laughs) Perhaps we could start with activities you have found enjoyable in the past.

Roger: Well, that is easy – football, tennis ... (pauses and looks away from Rebecca) not that any of them are possible because I can't keep up with any of my friends now anyway, so what's the point thinking about them?

Rebecca: Let's leave ruling anything out until later – keep trying to come up with activities you enjoy.

A few minutes later Roger was beginning to run out of ideas.

> *Rebecca:* Well, you may say bungee jumping is a daft suggestion, but never say never. Keep going, what about some really silly ideas?
> *Roger:* Comedy, I love going to see comedy. I could do with a laugh!
> *Rebecca:* Don't stop there, what else might make you laugh, perhaps that's important.
> *Roger:* Perhaps I could do stand-up myself – I was once Tweedledum in a school play!

Rebecca used a number of different strategies for helping Roger to get the most out of the brainstorming exercise. Initially, she encouraged him to include any option that came to mind, and later reminded him not to stop generating ideas until he was completely unable to come up with any more. In addition, she encouraged him not to judge any of his suggestions, and declined his invitation to dismiss one of his wilder propositions, and indeed encouraged him to search for more radical ones.

In any situation, once potential strategies have been identified they need to be assessed with a view to whether they can be successfully used and are likely to be a match for the goal. Health professionals can assist patients by helping them assess how confident they feel about putting the plan into action, as well as whether they feel it will work.

A detailed plan of action is also a very important element of success. Once some general strategies have been identified, a plan can be drawn up that might include reviewing the steps involved in achieving the plan and the sequence of those steps. It also involves specifying the resources and obstacles, and the knowledge and skills that might need to be acquired. These will all be specific to the goal involved. At times help will be needed from other people. In the case of new strategies, for example learning relaxation to help manage unpleasant procedures, some practice time may need to be included.

Evaluating the outcome

A vital part of any problem-solving process is the evaluation phase. Throughout the implementation of the action plan progress can be monitored and may even benefit from being recorded on paper. Checking whether the plan is being carried out as agreed and whether it is bringing the patient closer to the goal can help maintain motivation. This is particularly true when a series of sub-goals have been identified in order to achieve a superordinate goal.

In addition, continuous monitoring may help to highlight possible problems early in the implementation of the plan. The plan can then be reviewed and adjusted accordingly. Doing this early can help prevent the patient losing heart if they persist with a plan which turns out to be unsuccessful. Encouraging the patient to take credit for progress is important as it will enhance confidence when addressing any future difficulties. Equally identifying any mistakes and addressing them can help to increase the chances of success in the long term.

Once the plan has been fully implemented, the question is whether the goal has been achieved, and what impact it has had on the problem initially identified. Given the complexity of many of the situations faced by cancer patients, it is likely that the first attempts at solving the problem will not be sufficient. At this point, a review of the ways in which the problem solving has been effective and of the issues which remain outstanding can be useful. Revised plans for dealing with those problems can then be made in the same way as before. Sometimes, especially in situations where disease is progressing, the goals themselves may need to be revised or even the problem itself restated in more appropriate terms.

Developing the skills

Before helping patients to use goal-setting and planning strategies, you may want to get to grips with the strategies by trying them out for yourself. There is very good evidence that people who set goals for themselves are generally more satisfied with life, so it may provide you with greater benefits than improving your clinical practice. Perhaps by reading this book you have already set yourself a goal – improving your communication!

Conclusions

This chapter has focused on examining the basic building-block skills in some detail, the *how* to say it, and highlighted how they are used to implement the helping process outlined in the last chapter. The basic skills of active listening are used at almost every point in the helping process, and have particular value in establishing a relationship between you and your patient. Challenging skills are more commonly used when forming new perspectives, and goal-setting and planning skills come into their own once it is time to act to solve or ameliorate a problem.

In the next chapter we will move on to how these skills can be put to use in any meeting between a health professional and a patient, and in particular their specific use in a range of routine situations in cancer management. These will include delivering bad news and discussing emotional health with patients, as well as how they can be applied to more challenging situations, for example when patients develop symptoms of depression. The next two chapters will also look at the content of particular types of interview, the *what* to say, and how to draw on the skills and strategies we have been discussing to tackle some of the situations that health professionals and patients find most challenging.

Summary

- Particular communication skills can be learned and used to implement the different stages of the helping process.
- Active listening skills are the bedrock of the exploration stage, and allow you to understand the patient's views and convey your understanding and acceptance to them.
- Displaying behaviours that demonstrate your interest in what the patient is telling you is a key skill, and minimal encouragers such as nodding can help to convey that you are paying close attention.
- Close observation of the patient to identify both the factual content of the narrative, and the underlying emotional tone and any clues from non-verbal behaviour or inconsistencies all provide opportunities to develop a better understanding.
- Reflection, summarizing and paraphrasing provide structure to interviews allowing you to explore situations further, or acting as a form of punctuation to move the interview to a new topic.
- Open questions are designed to encourage patients to expand on their account of a situation, helping them to explain their thoughts further. In contrast focusing techniques, for example judiciously used closed questions, are used to check on specific issues, as is often required in assessing changes in symptoms.
- All of the skills involved in the exploration stage are relevant to the stage of developing new perspectives. In this stage such skills may be used differently to try to gain a different view of the problem to enhance the opportunities for constructive management of it.
- Providing timely and appropriate information is a key way to prompt patients to rethink situations, and its use in routine practice will be explored in more depth in chapter 6.
- Feeding back to patients the hunches or patterns observed can help to deepen their own understanding of the problem, and to highlight

---

unspoken thoughts about it that can inform the problem-solving process.

- Directly challenging patients' beliefs by encouraging them to explore how valid or helpful they might be, and actively generating alternative ways of considering the situation, are powerful techniques to move the patient into a new frame of reference for the problem.
- Challenging skills can be regarded as a hierarchy of tools that can help a person to gain a new perspective on and further insight into their problems. They comprise three elements:
  - provision of information
  - advanced empathy
  - tackling unhelpful thoughts, beliefs and assumptions.
- Information is most effective when it is tailored to the needs of the patient and given within a collaborative relationship. Asking about and clarifying what a patient knows already is the only strategy for establishing their level of information and understanding. Encouraging patients to self-monitor can be an effective means to collect information. Giving permission for questions to be asked will give the message that information will be shared.
- Advanced empathy is achieved when the implicit is made explicit. To consider what might be going on for the patient, take a step back and observe how the person is making you feel, identify themes and patterns in what the person is saying, check out inconsistencies and mixed messages; check out your hunches with the patient.
- To tackle unhelpful thoughts and assumptions: ask about underlying beliefs about a particular situation; explore the effect of unhelpful versus helpful thoughts; enquire about the evidence for these thoughts and assumptions; ask the patient to consider alternative explanations; highlight positive exceptions and strengths; where a patient cannot or will not revise their view of a situation gently confront them with your view and the likely consequences of them not changing.
- The third and final stage is to use goal-setting, planning and evaluation skills to bring about a solution to the identified problem. This process includes a feedback loop to help refine and improve the solution being applied. All the previously described skills can be brought to bear at this stage, but the addition of brainstorming to help generate effective solutions is crucial.

- All the skills at any stage can only be developed through practice and feedback. There are many informal and formal methods for learning the skills, and readers are encouraged to take any available opportunity to refine them.

Chapter Six

Managing Everyday Clinical Situations

A diagnosis of cancer and its subsequent treatment raise many issues. It is the significance of these issues for the individual that is a key factor in a person's adjustment and well-being. Moreover, as discussed in chapter 3, the meaning they hold for a person is a distillation of cultural, social and psychological factors.

To health professionals, often working under time pressure, it may seem that this individual meaning bears little relevance to the task of getting people seen, diagnosed and treated. However, without consideration and an understanding of the impact that cancer and its treatments have for individual patients, we will be unable to help them adjust to their disease. This in turn can give rise to misunderstandings, conflict and difficulties, for patient and health care professional alike.

This chapter looks at how you can integrate communication and counselling skills into everyday clinical practice. It is divided into three sections. The first looks at a number of core issues that remain relevant throughout a person's whole cancer journey and how to manage them. The second section lays out a general template for any clinical interview or interaction. The final section describes common concerns facing patients at key stages of their cancer journey, and demonstrates how, using the communication and counselling skills described in chapters 4 and 5, you can help clarify and prioritize these concerns with the patient and manage them.

Managing Core Issues

These issues are typically a blend of informational, practical, emotional and social factors. Keeping this in mind when discussing any aspect of a patient's care can help to guide you towards the most appropriate intervention. For solutions to be helpful they must fit the problem; there must be what the literature calls congruence. That is, there needs to be an explicit and agreed understanding of what the problem is prior to any solutions being explored. Take the example of someone who has just received their diagnosis. They are likely to have many questions about it (information issues), but also to be in a state of emotional turmoil (emotional issues). Giving the patient time on their own, with a relative or with a member of the medical team, to clarify and formulate what sort of information they need, may be of benefit at this stage. The health professional needs to check with their patients what their main concerns are and when the best time to deal with them would be.

Information issues

People naturally try and make sense of the information available to them and put it into some context. As patients we are 'common-sense' medical scientists who search for the meaning of our physical symptoms. Throughout the cancer journey there is the need for information. Crucially, however, the amount of information required for optimal adjustment differs from patient to patient. Identifying the problem as the patient sees it before offering information is therefore essential.

While this may sound obvious it is common for health professionals to make assumptions about the level of information and comprehension a patient possesses. This can undermine good communication, leaving patients confused and ill-equipped to deal with their situation and unable to participate fully in choices about their care. Reasons often given for not fully informing patients of what is happening, or likely to happen, include a lack of time, an assumption that they did not want to know or simply that they did not ask. However, most patients report not being given enough information by health professionals.

The following are some general guidelines for giving information:

- establish what the patient already knows and explore their view of the situation;
- explain what you are saying simply without using unnecessary medical jargon;
- group information into categories, such as what's wrong, investigations, treatment options and prognosis;
- be specific and give the most important information first. Do not overload the person with information;
- give the patient time to absorb the information;

- check the patient's understanding of what has been said;
- repeat or rephrase information if necessary;
- ask if there are any questions the patient would like to ask;
- repeat information and back it up with written or taped material;
- encourage the patient to note any questions they may have for subsequent meetings or agree who can be contacted regarding any further questions they may have.

Emotional issues

Asking about a patient's emotional well-being each time you meet is a useful barometer in assessing their ability to deal with a situation. Often professionals and patients collude in not acknowledging the emotional level. Patients can feel 'stupid' or that they are 'wasting your time' and so may elect not to raise their fears and concerns. Health professionals may also feel disinclined to ask about a person's emotional well-being, for fear of unearthing something that they feel ill-equipped to manage. However, this is ultimately counter-productive, as it excludes an important dimension of how someone is managing now as well as their ability to manage in the future.

After her treatment had finished, Gloria became frightened of coming to the hospital, since it brought back upsetting memories of her diagnosis and treatment which made her panic. Her fear became so great that she did not attend her follow-up appointments.

Once the reason underlying her non-attendance was addressed by the health care professional, it was possible for Gloria to talk about her thoughts surrounding the diagnosis and the overwhelming feelings and panic they evoked. She was then able to understand how these had become associated with the hospital and how her non-attendance had been a way of controlling these upsetting thoughts and feelings.

Only after the emotional level of care had been addressed did it become possible for Gloria to look at how this had come about and to discuss alternative strategies for dealing with attending follow-up appointments.

Practical issues

Establishing whether a person has the resources to respond to a situation may also be a key to understanding how they respond to their cancer and its treatment. The resources may include transport to get them to an early-morning appointment, someone to look after children during treatment, support with domestic chores, the energy to travel or the finances to consider stopping work. The practical realities faced by people with cancer can all have a profound effect on them. Inevitably information will be required, but in reality there may be the need for practical support. Health professionals are in a position to facilitate access to this by signposting other services.

People often struggle on with a difficult situation, either because they are unaware of assistance that may be available to them, or because they are reticent about asking for help. Here, health professionals can be a source of expert knowledge about the appropriateness of particular services and how to access them. Grants for help with expenses, assessment for adaptations and aids as well as help with personal care and domestic tasks can be useful. Assessment of the patient's practical concerns and a sensitive offer of help can be extremely valuable. A number of sources of practical help are listed at the end of the book.

Fran had to travel from Kent to central London for her radiotherapy every day for six weeks. She was initially given appointments in the early morning. She had tried to reschedule her appointments, but was told that the clinics were extremely busy and there was no later slot available. In order to get to her appointments on time she had to leave before 9.30 a.m. which meant having to pay the peak-rate fare which was a considerable drain on her finances. She felt unable to raise the issue again, as she could see the department was very stretched and she did not want to make a fuss.

There can be many reasons why patients do not receive the practical support they need. It is for health professionals to ensure that such issues are discussed as a matter of course.

Practical considerations are therefore important and should be incorporated into every episode of care, having due regard for the assertiveness and perseverance of the individual patient.

Social issues

A person's adjustment to their illness is also affected by how people around them adjust to the situation. Cancer and its treatments have repercussions for friends, family and work colleagues; they impact on the patient's social network. Finding out how a patient's social network is responding can be a useful indicator in assessing their own well-being. Encouraging discussion with and involvement of key relatives and the spouse or partner can help a person's psychological adaptation and well-being and help identify potential difficulties. Such involvement can also enable support for these key people to be addressed.

After Jack was advised that further treatment was no longer recommended, his family challenged this and requested a second opinion. Prior to his diagnosis it was to Jack that other family members turned in times of crisis. This made it difficult for him to express what he wanted to the family, as he felt he had to continue to be strong for them. A meeting between the medical team and Jack and his wife was set up, and it became clear that neither had raised the issues for fear of upsetting the other. They were able to see that this lack of communication was causing them to argue and were able to talk to the doctor about their individual worries and think how best to deal with them.

There is a dynamic relationship and interaction between emotional, informational, practical and social issues, with each one invariably having an impact on another. Patients may be facing a situation that raises difficulties at several levels. It is only by determining a clear idea of where a person stands in relation to these four domains that the health care professional is able to plan the most effective care with the patient.

Issues of uncertainty

Uncertainty is the hallmark of cancer and will be present in varying degrees throughout a person's cancer journey. From the moment of seeking advice about their symptoms, a person will be faced with many uncertainties. Each of these can be thought of as a potential threat, which can give rise to anxiety. This typically manifests itself as questions to do with the diagnosis and the success and consequences of treatment. Questions that are commonly asked include:

'Can it be treated?'
'Can it be cured?'
'What are the side effects of the treatment?'
'Will it come back?'

Such questions can be difficult for the health professional to cope with, but need to be addressed.

Uncertainty can make the health professional feel stressed and uneasy, although such feelings are not often openly acknowledged. Health professionals often possess a strong desire to help make people better. Therefore being confronted with situations where this may not be possible can cause distress. Health professionals often deal with such situations by what Maguire (1985) calls distancing – a process which can either inhibit the patient from disclosing their feelings or prevent them from being picked up. Such distancing tactics protect the health professional from having to contend with the patient's distress and also from situations in which they may feel ill-equipped to manage.

Ways in which health professionals distance themselves include avoiding the patient, not asking about the patient's emotions, ignoring cues about what is troubling them, premature reassurance, giving advice, focusing only on the positive aspects of treatment and playing down any side effects, and giving false hope. Each of these strategies risks undermining the integrity of the patient–health professional relationship.

In order to manage a patient's uncertainty it is crucial first to acknowledge it and to show empathy with the person's situation. Just being able to stay with and contain the patient's feelings surrounding any uncertainty can be helpful in enabling them to clarify what their worries are. From here the health professional and the patient can start to identify what may help. For example, one person may benefit from more information as a way of coping with their uncertainty, whereas another may find it helpful to talk about and ventilate their feelings. Without realizing and dealing with this emotional need, patients and health professionals can get caught in a seemingly never-ending cycle of questions and reassurances.

Guidelines for managing uncertainty

- Acknowledge the uncertainty and empathize with the feelings it arouses in the patient;
- be open about what you cannot answer;
- do not rush to do something;
- be aware of using distancing tactics;
- discuss what would help the patient deal with the uncertainty.

A Template for Meetings

Managing the key stages throughout the cancer journey requires giving thought not only to what is said, but to how it is said, when, where and by whom. It is useful to have a broad template for all meetings with patients. Having a structure will help you and your patient get most out of the meeting and enhance good communication. Such a template comprises the following elements:

- preparation
- introduction and opening
- agreeing an agenda and exploring issues
- prioritizing concerns
- taking action and looking forward
- closing.

Preparation

Communication between health professionals and patients can be influenced by events that occur before the meeting itself. For example, a patient who is anxious, as a result of not being able to locate a department easily, may be less able to assimilate information and make best use of their appointment. The receptionist's manner can also have a bearing on outcome, as they are often the first point of contact for the patient on arrival at the clinic. As Nick describes,

'No one seemed to have heard of the person I was due to see. I was sent to the wrong building first. I was in such a state by the time I arrived, I almost turned back home. To cap it all, the receptionist didn't seem to know who I was and proceeded to check all my details in earshot of the whole waiting-room. I was really upset and was made to feel it was all my fault. It wasn't what you'd call a good start.'

Thinking ahead to potential communications issues can help avoid unnecessary problems and reduce the conflict which arises when simple things go wrong, like a patient getting lost or being late for an appointment. Clear instructions and a map can help avoid unnecessary confusion and distress, as can a warm and helpful reception when patients arrive. This can best be achieved by clinicians and administrators working to plan systems which support good standards of communication, at both an organizational and an individual level.

Preparing at the organizational level When preparing for an appointment, a team approach is required to ensure that the patient's perspective is considered from their first contact with the service. Administrative staff can make a big impact on patients by the information they provide in advance of an appointment. In addition to simple attendance details, it is useful to state the name and role of the member of staff a patient will see and to include information about travel routes and times from key landmarks, how to confirm or rearrange the appointment if necessary, and how long the appointment will last. Patients might be encouraged to bring a friend or family member, and informed about how to prepare for the appointment. Where necessary this may state how to obtain information in languages other than English and the availability of translators. In the event of the patient attending the appointment for an investigation or treatment procedure, written information about what to expect can also be included.

All of the foregoing should serve to help the patient to plan their visit and to prepare psychologically for what may be a traumatic event. Moreover, apart from fostering operational efficiency, it will also have the effect of conveying respect to people visiting the organization you serve.

Preparing as a health care professional Good preparation is a sign that clinicians respect their patients. Patients find it upsetting to have to correct clinician's misunderstandings of their history. By contrast they are reassured when a health professional seems familiar with key events. Health professionals should read notes to familiarize themselves with the patient's history and current management, and do so in advance of the meeting wherever possible.

Finally, diverting telephone calls and putting a do-not-disturb sign up will help avoid interruptions. If other staff will be present, this needs to be explained to the patient. Similarly, permission should be sought when students attend consultations and this should be handled before the patient comes into the room.

All of the above preparation will convey the message to your patient that the meeting is important and that they have your undivided attention.

Introduction and opening

The first few moments of any meeting can colour how each party sees the other. The key at this stage is to put the patient at ease. Simply welcoming the patient into the room, shaking hands and introducing yourself and others present will help achieve this. Staying seated behind a desk and saying nothing until the person has sat down can convey a lack of interest and respect for them.

> 'When I walked into the room there was one chair right next to the desk. The doctor was on the phone and waved me in. I felt like a spare part waiting for him to come off the phone.'

A warm and interested manner gives the patient a good indication of your genuine concern. There is only one first impression and it is worth making it good.

Agreeing an agenda and exploring issues

The next task is to develop an agenda. This involves making clear the broad aims of the meeting as well as identifying any concerns that the patient may have, with a view to exploring them in more detail later. This is achieved through active listening and exploration to elicit a person's concerns.

Allowing patients time to say what has brought them to the meeting and what they hope to get out of it can be useful and is easily achieved by asking:

'What would you like to discuss?'
'What has brought you here today?'

Alternatively, where a referral has been made, you can start the meeting by stating your understanding of its purpose and go on to check whether that is in line with the patient's understanding.

'Dr Smith, your oncologist, has asked me to see you to discuss options for your chemotherapy treatment.'
'What's your understanding of coming to see me today?'

Usually there is more than one matter of concern to the patient. Using a follow-up question, such as:

'Is there anything else concerning you at the moment?' or
'Is there anything else you would like to discuss?'

can help to bring to light any additional worries or thoughts.

This simple strategy of agreeing the agenda allows you to quickly tune into the issues at stake for the patient, before moving on to explore specific issues in more detail.

Oncologist: So Mark, have you thought of any further things you would like to discuss about your diagnosis?

Mark: Not really.

Oncologist: Is there anything else on your mind?

Mark: Someone was telling me about what happens when you have treatment.

Oncologist: What about the treatment?

Mark: Well, side effects really.

Oncologist: What side effects in particular?

Mark: Being sick, I can't stand the idea of being sick all the time. My mate said his mother was sick for months because of her treatment.

The oncologist uses the initial stages of the interview to agree a mutual agenda for discussion and checks whether he has any further concerns before exploring them in more detail.

Prioritizing

Helping people to prioritize their concerns is the first step in identifying specific needs and generating solutions.

Health professionals are commonly under time pressure and telling the patient about the time available can help focus the meeting on what is most important. Where there seem to be more issues to discuss than time available, asking the patient to prioritize them into those that are urgent and those that could be left to a subsequent meeting can be helpful.

'We may not be able to cover all of the issues you've raised in the time we have today. Which do you want to deal with first?'

Encouraging patients to make a note of questions which come to mind before or in between consultations can also help them focus and make the most of the meeting.

Oncologist: So hearing about other people being sick during treatment is worrying you?

Mark: Too right!

Oncologist: Well, I'd be happy to explain the situation about that to you, but was there anything else you wanted to discuss?

Mark: Well, I've been wondering if I'm going to be able to work if I'm being sick all the time.

Oncologist: OK, so we need to talk about the chances of being sick, and your thoughts about how it might affect your work. (*summarizing*) Anything else?

Mark: Not really.

Oncologist: Fine. Well I'd like to discuss the results of the blood tests we did last time too. Which would you like to start with?

Here the oncologist, after identifying Mark's concerns, has summarized them and checked whether there are any further issues that Mark wishes to discuss. Having done this he has stated what he wants to discuss and asked Mark to prioritize his concerns.

Taking action and looking forward

Having established the areas of concern for the patient, the next stage of the helping process is to consider future possibilities. All of the skills that we have described above can be used at this stage of the interview, but there are additional strategies that are particularly suited to helping a patient to move ahead with an area of difficulty.

During this stage of the meeting, challenging and problem-solving skills come to the fore. These include:

- agreeing what the problem is;
- establishing and exploring a number of possible solutions;
- agreeing which solution or course of action is most appropriate at this stage.

Closing

A well-planned and -managed meeting should flow to a natural conclusion in the time allotted. Inevitably, people lose track of how far through the interview they are. Reminding patients of the time remaining can be useful.

'We have five minutes left, so perhaps we could agree. . . . '

Summarizing what has been discussed and agreed is also helpful in arriving at a logical closing point.

Applying Communication and Counselling Skills in Managing Everyday Clinical Situations

From the moment people experience symptoms they try to accommodate them into their model of the world. At each stage of their illness and treatment they will face a different set of issues. While the individual reality of cancer will vary for each person, there are common issues that arise at key stages in the course of their illness.

This section will describe how to manage these key stages and situations. It will also illustrate how to clarify what would be most helpful for the individual patient in each case. It is divided into six key areas, namely:

- initial consultation
- preparation for clinical procedures and investigations
- breaking bad news
- treatment options – helping with decision making
- ending treatment, including treatment failure
- follow-up.

At each of the above stages, the first task for the health care professional is to make clear the purpose of the meeting and to convey the qualities of an effective helper, described in chapter 4. These include warmth, respect and empathy, and shape the relationship within which the communication and counselling skills described in chapter 5 can be put to use.

Initial consultation

When patients present to their doctors, it is usually with a combination of signs and symptoms, of which they will have attempted to make some sense. Often they will have formed a hypothesis or model of what might be going on. In short a person's signs and symptoms are translated into an internal representation or illness representation. Such representations are influenced by other factors, as discussed in chapter 3 and can be thought of as the person's model of illness. Studies looking at these illness representations have concluded that they comprise five areas or 'dimensions' (Baumann et al. 1989; Leventhal et al. 1984). Together these give a useful insight into how a person views what is happening and the basis for that view (primary appraisal) as well as their beliefs about what they can do to control it (secondary appraisal).

> Sophie recalls her experience.
>
> 'I'd had a history of benign cysts – the last one being about 15 years ago – but this felt different. The GP kept saying that as the lump was malleable and painful it was nothing to worry about and yet I just knew that it wasn't the same as before. I instinctively felt that there was something wrong. I was so tired and felt unwell. But the GP – who was young enough to be my grandson – didn't even ask me what I thought it might be.
>
> 'I don't know why I didn't insist to be referred but I didn't want to cause a fuss. I did go back, but eventually my husband suggested I go privately. It was only after that consultation and mammogram it was suggested that I be referred to the breast unit.
>
> 'The tumour they found was 8cm and Grade 3. I keep thinking, why didn't anyone listen to me? No one ever asked me what I thought was happening. I get so upset when I think about it now; it's awful. I feel that there's nothing I can do any more.'

Given the proven significance of control and optimism (self-efficacy) in predicting adaptation and well-being, asking about the five dimensions listed below can give valuable insight into the information and reasoning behind a patient's hypothesis of what might be going on. The questions are taken from Faulkner and Maguire (1994).

1   The problem as the patient sees it (for example symptoms and what the person attributes these to).

 'What do you make of your symptoms?'

2   The cause of the problem (e.g. genetic, environmental, chance, stress).

 'Have you any theories about why you got cancer?'

3   The possible consequences of the problem (e.g. view of the self).

 'Has having had cancer diagnosed affected how you feel about yourself in any way?'

4   Expectations about the duration of the disease (e.g. acute or chronic, cured or dormant).

'How do you see your illness working out?'

5   Ideas about cure or controllability (e.g. ideas about what patients can do themselves and what the health care professional and the family can do to bring about recovery).

> *'Is there anything you feel you can do to combat your illness and contribute to your recovery/survival?'*
> *'How much support do you feel you've been getting from the doctors and nurses who are looking after you?'*
> *'How much support do you feel you've been getting from close friends and family since the diagnosis?'*

Patients will also have formed an idea as to what they want from the doctor, be it information and advice regarding a possible diagnosis, treatment, reassurance, tests or a referral-on for a specialist opinion or further investigation.

The task of an initial meeting, therefore, is not only to establish what is concerning the patient, but also to ascertain what their beliefs are about their signs and symptoms and what they want and expect from their helper. It is imperative for health care professionals not only to collect information, but also to facilitate the process by which the patient can be clear about what their presenting concerns are.

Illness representations (especially perceived consequences and perceived control) are important factors influencing medical (e.g. pain, glycaemic control), psychological (e.g. depression, self-esteem, anxiety, life satisfaction) and behavioural (e.g. working-time, impairment, activity-level) outcomes.

> Take Kate whose husband, Miles, had died of sarcoma the year before her diagnosis of breast cancer. Following a lumpectomy she complained of pain and numbness in her arm and was fearful of radiotherapy being administered to her armpit.
>
> *Kate:* I worry about the pain and numbness in my arm. I keep thinking about Miles. After his operation he lost all movement and sensation in his left arm on account of the hospital severing a nerve.
> *Oncologist:* So what do you think your pain and numbness may be about?
> *Kate:* Well everyone tells me it's normal after the operation to experience numbness but I worry whether the same thing has happened to me. It's my left arm that's affected too just like Miles and his never recovered. In fact no one bothered to tell us what had happened to his arm during the surgery.

(cries)

Oncologist: So you worry that your arm may not recover like Miles's?

Kate: Well yes, and the thought of radiating that area is just too awful to think about, but I've got to make a decision.

Oncologist: It sounds as though there are several things worrying you at the moment and making it difficult for you to come to a decision about radiotherapy.

Kate: Yes. I don't want to be a nuisance but. . . . (cries)

Oncologist: It's clearly upsetting you (*reflection*) and I can understand your concerns. (*empathy*) What would help you in coming to a decision about treatment? (*looking forward*)

Here, simply through asking Kate what she believes her symptoms to be about, the doctor has quickly tuned into her fears that her arm may not recover and may have been damaged as was her husband's. By actively listening to and acknowledging Kate's distress when talking about Miles, the doctor has also identified another area of concern – that of radiotherapy to her armpit. This has opened the way to find out what would help her in dealing with this worry. For example, this might include information about her operation, the normal after-effects and what she could do to deal with the symptoms. It might also involve emotional support to help her deal with what happened to her husband.

Preparation for procedures and investigations

The prospect of undergoing investigations provokes anxiety in most patients. There is considerable research evidence to show that where patients are informed in advance about the investigations, they cope better, recover more quickly and need less pain relief (Ley 1982; Nichols 1984).

Jo recalls her colonoscopy.

'The nurse showed me into the clinical examination room and told me to get undressed from the waist down and put on a gown. I had an idea of what the examination was going to entail and wasn't exactly looking forward to it. I remember feeling pretty nervous and embarrassed about it in equal measure.

'When the doctor came in, he shook my hand and introduced himself. He put me at ease straight away, by asking me whether I had had a colonoscopy before and what I knew about the procedure. Before he examined me, he sat down and explained what he would be doing and showed me the tube that would be inserted. He warned me that it may be uncomfortable and a little painful but that would pass and suggested that I took a few deep breaths to help me relax during the examination. Before starting he asked if I had any questions.

'Throughout the procedure he talked me through what was happening, which was really reassuring and helpful. It's not the nicest thing to go through but he managed the situation really well. Focusing on the breathing had the effect of taking my mind off what was happening and gave me something to do. In fact it wasn't as painful as I thought it was going to be. Afterwards he asked me to get dressed and come through into the adjoining room to discuss what would happen next and answer any questions I might have. Throughout he treated me like an intelligent human being.'

In the above case the doctor helped Jo feel at ease by following a few simple guidelines. At first he introduced himself and then gave a clear explanation about what the investigation entailed, thus establishing the agenda, before embarking upon the examination. In doing so he demonstrated empathy and respect for Jo, which put her at ease. He suggested something she could focus on (i.e. breathing) during the examination to help her manage the pain and discomfort. Throughout the investigation the doctor kept Jo informed about what was happening, which reduced her anxiety and increased her sense of control. Finally, after the examination he allowed her to get dressed in privacy and then finished the consultation in a separate room, giving Jo an opportunity to ask questions.

When the following guidelines have been used, patients have reported less fear:

- Information about the procedure is given and understanding about it checked.

    'You are having an endoscopy today. This involves passing a small tube like this down the oesophagus to the opening of the stomach.'

- The somatic sensations of the investigation are described in clear, concrete language.

    'When the tube is passed down through your oesophagus you will experience discomfort and the desire to gag.'

- The sensations are identified as benign and non-threatening.

  'It may feel quite uncomfortable but that is normal and nothing to worry about.'

- A plan of action is discussed as to what the patient could do to cope with or control any unpleasant sensations.

  'You might find it helpful to concentrate on your breathing.'

- Where possible verbal contact is maintained with the patient as they undergo the procedure, encouragement given and effective use of coping strategies reinforced.

  'This might feel uncomfortable . . . the tube is now in place . . . well done! . . . you're doing really well.'

It is important to make time for patients to raise any queries or concerns that they may have, the key objective being to give them an opportunity for control.

The purpose of preparation is to reposition the meaning of these perceptual experiences from threatening to benign, so as to enable the patient to adapt their coping style. When a patient is informed about what to expect they are able to develop a clear picture of the procedure and to focus what they can do to manage the situation practically (e.g. relax) and emotionally (e.g. reassure themselves).

Breaking bad news

A person will receive bad news at least once in their experience of cancer. Thought needs to be given to what is told, when it is told, where it is told, how it is told and who breaks the news. Good planning and sufficient time are key to easing the receipt of bad news.

Caroline describes how she was told that she had cancer.

'I was called into the consulting room and the doctor I had seen for my initial investigations was there with some medical students I think. He said he was sorry, but that my investigations had shown that there was a malignant tumour in my ovaries and then talked about surgery and treatment. I remember hearing the word malignant and thinking all sorts of things all at once. I just felt removed from the situation; I could hear the doctor talking, but I couldn't take in what he was really saying; I was just so shocked; I just kept thinking I've got cancer and that I'd never have children.

'He asked me if I had any questions and I didn't really know what to ask, although at the same time my head was full of questions. In the end I just wanted to get out and be on my own to take it all in. Eventually he said that I would be contacted about a date for surgery and that a follow-up appointment would be made for me. He wrote some things in the notes and then I left.'

Here the doctor did not introduce the people present and failed to orientate Caroline as to the broad aims and running order of the meeting. When he gave the diagnosis, the doctor did not check Caroline's understanding of the term 'malignant' and failed to explore her immediate concerns about fertility. Instead he went on to talk about surgery. Consequently, he did not pick up that she was unable to attend to what he was saying, as she was in a state of shock and unable to articulate her immediate concerns. At this point Caroline split off from the situation. In closing the meeting the doctor missed the opportunity to summarize and check Caroline's understanding of what had been discussed and agreed. No further appointment or information about back-up support was given, to allow her to explore her thoughts and feelings about the diagnosis, her treatment options and any other concerns. In summary, the lack of agreed structure to the meeting and the absence of basic counselling skills resulted in Caroline feeling both anxious about and excluded from the situation.

Initially the shock of being diagnosed as having cancer may be overwhelming. This emotional reaction may make it difficult to assimilate information and yet it is usually the time when decisions about treatment options (e.g. surgery) are raised and also required. In the above case, Caroline's emotional response hijacked the consultation, leaving her unable to take in what the doctor was saying. In a study funded by the Cancer Research Campaign (CRC 1998) that looked at the retention of information in women receiving a diagnosis of breast cancer, it was found that after the diagnosis had been given the women could only recall two pieces of information.

It has also been demonstrated that patients who view the information given as adequate to their needs, adapt better to being given a diagnosis of cancer. Again this fits with the importance of appraisal in predicting a person's response. It is important, then, to ask what they know and understand of their diagnosis and what they want to know. This allows the solution to fit the problem and so promotes congruence.

Guidelines for breaking bad news

The following set of guidelines is designed to help those breaking bad news.

Be prepared – orientate yourself
- Provide a suitable setting where you will not be interrupted by telephones or other people;
- allow time – feeling rushed will not help you or your patient;
- read the notes before seeing the patient;
- have a strategy; know what you want to say and rehearse it.

Orientate the patient
- Greet the patient and introduce yourself, if you have not met previously, and anyone else present;
- explain the purpose and running order of the meeting and check this against the patient's expectations.

Deliver the news
- Explore the patient's prior expectations of the results (aligning);
- give a brief résumé of the tests carried out;
- give the results. Explain what they mean, simply and clearly. Avoid unnecessary jargon; explain any technical terms and check that the person understands what you are saying. It may be necessary to repeat the news;
- give the patient time to take the news in and yourself time to observe their reaction;
- acknowledge the patient's distress and encourage any expression of emotion, however strong, and do not rush to stop it. Inquire about feelings if none are expressed;
- ask the patient if they have any questions and answer them where possible. Feel able to say you do not know, but offer to find more information, if appropriate;
- acknowledge the patient's need to clarify their thoughts and feelings about the diagnosis and discuss how they may do that (for example on their own or with a specialist nurse).

Close the meeting
- Acknowledge the need to bring the meeting to a close;

- summarize what has been discussed;
- repeat the key information. Cluster bits of information to help retention. Back up verbal information with fact sheets or tapes;
- explain that it is normal not to have everything sorted, and that some time to assimilate what has been discussed may be helpful;
- before the end of the meeting check if there are any outstanding questions that the person would like to ask;
- clarify what the patient needs and what would be most helpful for them now;
- identify support systems/mechanisms with the patient (e.g. someone to talk to). Explain what other resources are realistically available (e.g. information, help-lines);
- explain what will happen from here regarding follow-up appointments and provide a point of contact, ideally an individual person;
- arrange a further session to allow the patient the opportunity to go over the diagnosis and ask questions;
- note what has been discussed with the patient and the agreed plan of action. Ensure that the appropriate staff are informed of this.

Treatment options

Patients offered a choice of treatments appear to adjust better than those who are not (Morris and Royle 1988). However, this is often an area where patients report not feeling involved sufficiently in the decision-making process regarding their treatment. This can be for a number of reasons. It may be that the person has insufficient or incorrect information about the various treatment options, which precludes them from making an informed decision. They may be reluctant to ask about different treatment options for fear of alienating their doctor; they may be confused and unclear about what they think and feel about the various options. Finally there may be a practical reason such as not having had the time to fully discuss the implications of the various treatments.

Following her diagnosis of breast cancer Jan, aged 31 years, described her meeting with her surgeon to discuss treatment options.

'He told me what they had found and that it was cancer and that I needed a mastectomy. I asked him about other less radical options but he just said that in his opinion that was the best course of action. He was quite abrupt and hardly looked at me when talking. I felt really upset but tried to keep calm. Then I asked him if I could have a reconstruction. He said that he wouldn't perform one but didn't really say why not. He did say he could bring me in to have the operation the next week. I was so stunned and beginning to feel really panicky at the thought of having to have a mastectomy and to decide what to do there and then. It was awful.'

Here the surgeon did not make explicit the purpose of their meeting, that is, to discuss and agree treatment options. Rather, he gave his opinion as to his preferred option and did not explain the reasoning behind this. When Jan asked about other options, he did not explore her concerns and therefore was unable to address them. His manner and poor active-listening skills (i.e. lack of eye contact, failure to summarize and check) meant that he failed to notice Jan's concern and gave Jan the impression that he was abrupt and unwilling to involve her in the choice of treatment.

Patients usually want to discuss possible treatment options with their doctor. It is best to make a separate appointment to discuss these.

The point of diagnosis is not the time to expect a person to make decisions about their treatment; they are likely to be upset and unclear about what they want to know. Thought also needs to be given to what information a patient needs to have in order to make a decision, and to who will provide this.

In order for the patient to make an informed decision about treatment, the following aspects will need to be covered:

- What are the various options, including no treatment?
- What does each entail (i.e. what is the mode of treatment and when will it happen)?
- How long will it last, where will it be carried out and who will perform it?
- What are the known outcomes and side effects of each?
- What, if any, is the health professional's preferred option and why?

There is more to this process than simply running through the checklist; the health care professional needs to establish the patient's understanding of the various options and seek to clarify their thoughts about any consequences of the treatments.

In coming to a decision a patient also needs to process the information (i.e. make sense of it in relation to themselves). To facilitate this the health professional can encourage the patient to:

- explore their thoughts and feelings about each option;
- identify the pros and cons of each option and prioritize these in order of importance;

● discuss the options with spouse, partner, friend or relative.

Aged 35, Emma had been diagnosed with and treated for breast cancer, undergoing a lumpectomy and axillary node clearance (i.e. removal of the lymph nodes) followed by chemotherapy and radiotherapy. Throughout she had been worried about possible infertility and what implications this might have for her relationship. She had maintained menstruation throughout her chemotherapy and was now being offered a two year course of Zolidex injection hormone therapy in addition to the five-year tamoxifen oral hormone therapy.

Nurse: You seemed upset when talking about whether or not to take Zolidex in addition to tamoxifen. Is it important for you at the moment?

Emma: Yes, I think about it all the time and then get really upset. I just don't know what to do. I feel so unsure and keep changing my mind; then I feel like I'm wasting everyone's time. (bursts into tears)

Nurse: I don't think you're wasting everyone's time – it's obviously something that's upsetting you (*empathy*) and it sounds like you have mixed feelings about the treatment. (*reflection of content and emotion*)

Emma: That's just how I feel; all mixed up.

Nurse: Perhaps it would help to clarify your feelings about it?

Emma: Yes, but I've been through all the information and still don't know what to do for the best. My thoughts just keep going round in circles and I'm no further forward with a decision.

Nurse: It sounds as though you know the facts but are still unclear in your own mind as to how you feel about them.

Emma: (cries)

Nurse: . . . and that's making you upset. (*reflection of feeling*)

Emma: So how do I start to sort it all out?

Nurse: Would it be helpful to look at the pros and cons of Zolidex?

Emma: Yes, maybe.

Nurse: You sound unsure.

Emma: Well that's just it – I'm unsure about everything. Sorry, I would like to look at the options and get my thoughts clear about them once and for all.

Nurse: OK, we can arrange that. You've mentioned several worries today about Zolidex, including the possibility of an induced menopause, the fear of infertility in the future and how that might affect your relationship. (*summarizing*) Before we next meet it would be helpful to write down any other worries you have about Zolidex. In that way we can go through them one by one. How does that sound? (*checking*)

Emma: Yes, I think that could be a good idea.

Here the nurse has acknowledged Emma's anxiety surrounding her decision about a particular treatment option. Through a process of reflection, summarizing and checking she has identified the main issues affecting Emma's decision. This has enabled them to agree that, despite having the information about the treatment, Emma has not processed her thoughts and feelings about it fully. By picking up on this emotional level of need they have been able to agree a way forward to solve it.

End of treatment

Treatment can come to an end for a number of reasons, such as completion of the regime, adverse reactions and relapse. Whatever the reason, ceasing treatment can be a time when patients feel frightened and vulnerable. After the distraction of dealing with the various aspects of their treatment, this can be a time when they contemplate how to cope with life. 'I can't believe I'd ever be upset at not coming to this place again. But in an odd way I feel safe because I'm being kept an eye on.' Where treatment has come to an end prematurely, patients can feel upset and anxious. Worries about recurrence and their future health are common at the end of treatment.

To help patients with this transition, it is helpful to do the following:

- review treatment progress, including outcome so far and, where appropriate, the reasons for stopping treatment prematurely;
- ask how they see their illness in the future;
- ask about any worries they have – emotional, informational, practical and social;
- discuss how they might manage their particular worries and what could help them cope;
- provide information on other support services and where appropriate discuss and arrange referral;
- agree a contingency plan for how and who to contact if they have any worries that can't wait until their next appointment.

Follow-up

Follow-up appointments allow the treatment plan to be monitored and evaluated. This is a time when the initially expected outcomes can be evaluated. For patients it can be an opportunity to raise any concerns and to receive feedback and reassurance on their progress. However, the meeting may serve as a reminder of their illness and can therefore also be an anxiety-provoking experience, throwing up mixed emotions. The agenda for follow-up meetings can be unclear. The health professional is often looking for absence of complications, whereas the patient is seeking reassurance that they are doing well.

Martin comes into the room with two doctors.

Doctor: (sitting) How have you been since our last appointment?

Martin: Not too bad. I'm still uncomfortable from the surgery and it's still very painful passing urine – as if there's still a blockage.

Doctor: Well we've had your blood results and I think it would be good to start you on hormone treatment as soon as possible which should ease things and help you pass urine.

Here the opportunity to clarify what is concerning Martin most is missed. The doctor has not explained the purpose of the meeting and hence what is expected. The patient responds to an open question with a series of concerns that are not picked up on. The opportunity to establish Martin's existing level of and need for information about his symptoms, his emotional concerns and practical needs (e.g. pain relief), has been missed.

It is important to orientate the patient about the purpose and running order of the meeting, and what is expected from them, at the outset. This helps focus the meeting.

Martin is called into the room.

Doctor: Hello Martin. Please come in and take a seat. This is Dr Jones, the Registrar on the team, who is sitting in with me today. I understand that you're happy for her to be here?

Martin: Yes, the nurse asked me before I came in and that's fine. You've got to learn somewhere.

Doctor: Thank you. Now it's been two weeks since your surgery. What I'd like to do today is to check on your progress, examine you and then discuss possible treatment options with you. Before I begin is there anything in particular that you want to discuss or that's worrying you?

Martin: Well I'm worried about not being able to pass urine very easily. It's so painful, it feels as if there's still a blockage there like before. Is that normal?

Doctor: It is very common in the first couple of weeks after surgery on the prostate for patients to report pain on urination. One reason for this is that while the site is healing blood clots can get passed through the urethra in the urine. This can be very painful and feel as if there is something blocking the

> flow, but in fact it is the clot being passed causing that sensation.
>
> *Martin:* So it's nothing to worry about then?
>
> *Doctor:* For the first few weeks no. This is quite normal following surgery and it should settle as the wound heals.
>
> *Martin:* Right, that makes sense.
>
> *Doctor:* Have you any other concerns? What are they?
>
> *Martin:* Yes – well, about when I should be able to go back to work. I've already had a few weeks off.
>
> *Doctor:* It's difficult to be prescriptive. Everyone's different. It depends on several things really. Could we come back to that after I've had a look at you and assessed your progress?

Here the doctor has put the patient at ease by greeting him courteously and orientating him to the purpose of the meeting. He has not only given permission for the patient to raise any concerns but also successfully managed the order of the meeting.

The following is a list of tips on how to manage follow-up meetings:

- prepare the patient beforehand about the purpose of the meeting. This can be done verbally at discharge and backed up with written information about the nature of the meeting (i.e. discussion, examination, investigations);
- greet the patient as he or she comes into the room and introduce yourself and others where appropriate. Explain the purpose of the meeting, the time available and the areas you would like to or need to cover;
- ask if there is anything that the patient would like to raise before the meeting begins, suggest a running order for the meeting and indicate that there will be time for questions;
- discuss and explain any clinical findings and your opinion regarding the progress and management with the patient. Signal to the patient when you are about to discuss their case with any students or colleagues who may be present.
- throughout the meeting seek to clarify the patient's care needs, along the four dimensions informational, emotional, practical and social. Highlight what the patient can do to help their situation;
- agree the plan of action;
- summarize what has been agreed. It may be helpful for the patient to note this down to help them remember later;
- ask if there are any outstanding questions or issues that the patient would like to raise;

- explain what will happen next regarding future contact;
- provide a contact for any interim concerns;
- make a note of what has been discussed and communicate this to relevant members of the care team.

Conclusions

A patient's adaptation will depend on their appraisal of the situation and what they feel can be done to control it. By employing good communication and counselling skills, health care professionals can discover a patient's key concerns and, importantly, find out what will help them to manage these. Adequate planning and consistency in approach and questioning style are two of the hallmarks of success and the reader is invited to utilize the practical tools set out in this chapter to achieve it.

Summary

- Issues facing people with cancer are typically a blend of informational, emotional, practical and social factors.
- Health care professionals work collaboratively with patients to gather information and agree priorities in several key areas: managing uncertainty, identifying information needs, assessing emotional well-being and addressing practical needs.
- Involving key relatives, spouses and partners can help facilitate psychological adaptation.
- Having a template for meetings is worthwhile. Here is a typical structure:
  Preparation: Give clear instructions to the patient regarding time, place and what to expect. Read notes before the meeting. Ensure privacy and minimize interruptions.
  Introduction and opening: Make the right impression. Show interest in and respect for the patient. Put the patient at ease as this will help establish rapport. Be clear about the purpose of the meeting.
  Agreeing agenda: Set and agree the topics to be discussed. Invite the patient to add any additional topics for discussion.
  Prioritizing: Make use of limited time by prioritizing key issues for discussion with the patient.

Taking action and looking forward: Consider all the options open to the patient. The skills of problem solving and challenging are particularly helpful in moving things forward. Agree an action plan and how this will be followed up (e.g. agree the date of the next meeting or feedback).

Closing: Leave enough time to close the meeting properly. Summarize what has been discussed and agreed. Allow time for questions.

- While the individual reality of cancer will vary for each person there are common issues that arise over the course of the illness. Health care professionals have devised practical guidelines for managing these issues which fall into six main areas:

Initial consultation: establish what is concerning the patient and what he or she wants. Ask about how the patient interprets his or her symptoms and illness (i.e. illness representation). This comprises five domains (i) the problem as the patient sees it; (ii) the cause of the problem; (iii) possible consequences of the problem; (iv) the expected duration of the illness; (v) the cure and controllability of the illness.

Preparation for investigations: give clear information about what to expect and what the patient can do to control any unpleasant sensations. This reduces distress and enhances well-being.

Breaking bad news: ensure organizational and individual planning, orientate the patient, ask about expectations, give results and key information, acknowledge and contain distress.

Treatment options: discuss all options with the patient and give them the time and information to decide. Include the patient and significant others in the decision-making process.

End of treatment: help with transition and mixed feelings. Review progress. Help the patient identify future coping strategies and support systems. Provide a person to contact.

Follow-up: set a date to monitor and evaluate progress.

Chapter Seven

Recognizing and Managing Difficult Situations

So far we have looked at everyday clinical communication throughout the cancer journey and the skills that can help to foster good communication and promote a sense of well-being. This may be all that is required to help a person adapt to the changes that their cancer presents. But what happens when things do not go according to plan? Adjustment to change is not always easy and there will be times when you will need to use all the skills described in chapter 5, with particular emphasis on those of challenging.

In this chapter we will look at situations that health professionals commonly identify as difficult. We will give some general guidelines about how to manage these situations and, finally, illustrate these and the use of challenging skills in a series of case studies.

The sorts of situations that healthcare professionals often describe as difficult tend to be categorized around a description of the patient (e.g. distressed, angry, anxious, depressed, suicidal, demanding or where they are facing multiple losses or other trauma). This is over-simplistic and implies it is the patient, rather than the situation, that is difficult. We suggest that it is the feelings raised, rather than the patients, that are difficult for health professionals to manage.

For people with cancer, feelings of fear, anger, depression, helplessness, resentment, sadness, grief, shame and embarrassment are commonplace. In life we all experience these emotions and develop ways of protecting ourselves from the distress they can cause; we develop defences, that is, ways of behaving and thinking which allow us to avoid facing uncomfortable feelings. However, when feelings are not expressed and acknowledged, misunderstandings and conflict can arise and this is unhelpful for everyone concerned. As a rule, where patients are given permission to express their emotions and responded to with empathy, potentially difficult situations can be managed more effectively. In general, this involves the helper forming a view of the world through their patient's eyes, assessing the validity of that view and using a different set of tools to encourage the person to re-evaluate their model of the world.

Before looking at specific situations in detail, here are some general guidelines that can be helpful in managing any difficult clinical situation:

- Acknowledge any difficulty or impasse and ask about the patient's feelings.
- Accept what patients say they are feeling; do not challenge it.
- Try and see the situation from the patient's point of view and do not take what is said personally.
- Stand back and reflect on what might be happening. Ask yourself, 'What is going on here?' There is always a reason why someone is behaving or feeling as they do.
- Use your own feelings as a barometer to gauge what the patient may be feeling. Simply ask yourself 'What does the patient make me feel?', for example anxious, irritated, overwhelmed, helpless and if so, why?
- Clarify and separate out which feelings belong to whom.
- Look for triggers or antecedents of the behaviour and put it into context. Assessing a patient in their entirety can help decipher whether this is normal for them or whether there has been a change in some way.
- Once you have identified the emotion, try and generate some hypotheses as to why the person might be feeling the way they do. This is sometimes called the 'ABC' approach:
  - What is the trigger?   Antecedent   (A)
  - What actually happens?   Behaviour   (B)
  - What is the outcome?   Consequences   (C)
- Check out your hunches with the patient. Ask them what they think is going on, as a way of including them in the process.
- Identify underlying beliefs and assumptions about the situation:
  - gently challenge assumptions, attitudes and mixed messages;
  - discuss their validity and helpfulness with the patient;
  - look at alternative explanations.
- Try and get the patient to focus on what they could do to make things better (enhancing their self-efficacy); refer to the here and now and ask:

  'What would be most helpful now?', and
  'What could you or others do to make things better?'

Everyone's cancer journey is different, so it is important not to stereotype patients. Nevertheless, in order to illustrate some of the key strategies that are helpful in managing difficulties, we will now illustrate these in a series of clinical situations that health professionals have identified as difficult to deal with.

Case Studies Illustrating Difficult Clinical Situations

The distressed patient

Being confronted with a distressed patient often triggers strong feelings in the health professional who might find them difficult to deal with. Common concerns for helpers include a fear of being overwhelmed themselves and of being incompetent to deal with such strong emotions. However, these feelings provide clues as to how your patient may be feeling, and when made explicit can help them reappraise the situation. In order to do this, be aware of feelings that a patient arouses in you, through thinking,

'How does this person make me feel?'

and use this to check if that is how the patient is feeling.

Being able to empathize with the person at a deeper level should in turn strengthen the helper relationship and make it appropriate to challenge the person's beliefs and overall appraisal of their situation and enable them to consider new perspectives.

For example, a patient feeling overwhelmed on receiving bad news may well project their feelings onto the person delivering the message. This can in turn leave the health professional feeling overwhelmed and at a loss as to how to help. Realizing that what you are feeling may be a reflection of how the patient feels can be very helpful in understanding what the person is going through. This is something that can easily be checked out:

'It must be a shock for you.'

Articulating your feelings not only allows patients to crystallize and realize what they are experiencing, but may also demonstrate an understanding of their viewpoint. Generally speaking, it helps to identify and locate feelings before giving advice and direction or challenging patients to reappraise their situation.

As a way of protecting themselves from such discomfort, some carers distance themselves and ignore clues that the patient gives. While this may make the health care professional feel better and more in control, such responses have the opposite effect for the patient, as Anne's case illustrates.

> *Doctor:*   Hello Anne, come in and sit down. I understand that when you were
> last at clinic, it was suggested that we carry out some blood tests to check out
> when your next treatment could start and that's what I'd like to discuss with
> you today. Before we look at those, how have you been since we last met?
> *Anne:*   I'm just so tired all the time. (bursts into tears) I'm sorry. And I can't
> seem to stop crying.
> *Doctor:*   It must be difficult but things will get better – really. The good news is
> that your counts are up and we can get on with your next chemotherapy
> treatment and hopefully it'll all be through by Christmas. You will feel tired
> but it should get better and I'm sure everything else will fall into place.

While acknowledging Anne's difficulty, the doctor here prematurely reassures
her that things will improve. This is done without exploring the causes of her
distress. Anne's tears and her mention of feeling tired are responded to with
a general platitude that things will improve. The opportunity to discuss possible reasons for her upset has been lost.

Such strategies have the effect of inhibiting disclosure on the part of the
patient with the risk of it escalating and erupting at a later date.

In the following example, the doctor acknowledges and stays with Anne's
distress, resisting the urge to reassure her. In doing so, he enables Anne to
regain control and go on to talk about the underlying causes of her distress.
This enables them to get to the point where they can think about how Anne
might resolve these.

> *Anne:*   I'm just so tired all the time. (bursts into tears) I'm sorry. And I can't
> seem to stop crying.
> *Doctor:*   That's all right. Do you want to talk about it? (*gentle encouragement*)
> *Anne:*   I'm worried about being so tired all the time and not having the energy
> to do anything properly.
> *Doctor:*   What sort of things? (*focusing*)
> *Anne:*   Well, everything really; housework, helping the kids with their home-
> work and stuff. At the end of the day I'm so tired, then I get irritable with the
> children, and it's not their fault. (cries) I just feel it's not fair on them.
> They've been through so much and for me to be bad tempered on top of all
> that isn't fair.
> *Doctor:*   It's as if you feel guilty about being tired and not being able to do
> things – especially with the children. (*advanced empathy through making the implicit
> explicit*)
> *Anne:*   Yeah, that's it – I feel guilty about everything.
> *Doctor:*   It sounds as though you're expecting yourself to carry on as before, but

maybe that's not possible right now given how tired you've been feeling with the chemotherapy. (*challenging assumptions*)

Anne: Yeah, but what can I do about it?

At this point, after having contained Anne's distress and encouraged her to explore the triggers of it in more depth, the doctor has been able to help Anne see how her tiredness, irritability and guilt link together. By demonstrating empathy and putting forward an alternative explanation as to what might be going on, the doctor has enabled Anne to question (i.e. challenge) the viability of her current strategy of carrying on as normal. This has in turn helped Anne to move to the point where she is ready to look at other ways (new perspectives) of dealing with the situation.

As we saw in chapters 4 and 5, the first stage of helping is to actively listen and help explore the problem. To do this the health professional needs to provide an environment that allows the patient both to talk about their thoughts and feelings and to feel safe in doing so. Staying with and containing the patient's distress can be extremely helpful in itself, as it both normalizes the experience and encourages further exploration and disclosure.

This is a crucial first step in helping the person to deal with their distress, but is not necessarily easy, since exploring these issues can often feel threatening to patient and health professional alike.

The angry patient

Anger is a difficult emotion to manage. The reasons for this often go back to our childhood. As children expressing anger, we were often told by adults, 'Stop that', or 'Don't be rude', and 'Pull yourself together'. For this reason, anger is often labelled as negative. Children can grow up believing that it is unacceptable to feel and express anger, and become unable to express it appropriately. Rather, they either erupt or bottle things up and withdraw. Anger can also be the outward expression of a different underlying emotion, such as fear.

When people do express anger those around them often feel threatened and can respond by becoming defensive, antagonistic, or deliberately avoiding any confrontation. In clinical settings one outcome is that the patient's anger is not acknowledged and the opportunity to explore the underlying cause may be lost.

We now consider three ways in which anger commonly arises in clinical settings:

- justifiable anger
- displaced anger
- aggression.

Justifiable anger There will be times when patients are justifiably angry, for example about how the system operates and the way that they are treated. Working within the health system, professionals can become immune to issues such as mislaid notes, long waiting times and errors. For the patient, however, such events can be very distressing, and the health professional's apparent lack of concern can come across as uncaring.

> *Patient:*   This just isn't on. I've been waiting for an hour and I demand to see the supervisor.
> *Radiotherapist:*   Everyone has had to wait today. I'm sorry but there's nothing we can do and getting upset won't alter anything. Please sit down and you'll be seen as soon as possible.
> *Patient:*   But I always have a long wait. It's not good enough! You just don't seem to care that we all have to sit here on these excruciatingly uncomfortable chairs while you swan around. By the time I get seen transport will have packed up and gone.
> *Radiotherapist:*   I can assure you we're not swanning around, Mr Smith. A machine has broken down and we're doing our best given the situation. You will be seen today. It's a case of being patient, I'm afraid.

In the above exchange the radiotherapist has failed to pick up on this patient's feelings. Instead, he has reacted defensively to what the patient has said (factual content) rather than listening to how it has been said (emotional content). In so doing, the radiotherapist has closed the door to exploring what might help. The patient has raised several concerns, including the long wait, the uncomfortable seating and worries about transport. He is clearly both angry and anxious.

Perhaps this would have been a better way of handling matters:

> *Radiotherapist:*   I can see and understand you're angry about the delay. (*acknowledges and empathizes using reflection of emotion*)
> *Patient:*   Well you'd be too.
> *Radiotherapist:*   Yes. (*nods, i.e. validates with self-disclosure*) I apologize for the long delay and the inconvenience. Due to an earlier machine breakdown there have been long delays today. We're trying to be as quick as we can. There are two people to be seen before you and so I think it will be another 15 or 20 minutes before you're called. What about any other concerns? (*open question*)

Patient: Well, will transport wait for me?

Radiotherapist: If you're worried about transport, I can call them to explain the situation if that would help? (*looking at options*)

Patient: Yes, I'd appreciate that. I don't want to find that they've all gone home or have another long wait. If you could let them know what's happening that would be great. Thank you.

Here the radiotherapist has acknowledged the patient's anxiety and empathized with how he is feeling rather than contesting what is being said. This has had the effect of maintaining the relationship and keeping the channels of communication open, which has enabled the underlying causes of the patient's anger and anxiety to be pinpointed and possible solutions to be discussed and agreed.

Displaced anger Where patients do not direct their feelings at the person or situation causing it, these feelings can become displaced (i.e. focused on a seemingly unrelated event or person). For health care professionals such displays of anger can seem out of proportion, unjustified and difficult to manage.

In such situations it is helpful to step back and see what else might be fuelling the anger. To do this it is important to remain objective and non-judgemental. This will maintain the helping relationship by keeping the channels of communication open, enabling further exploration of the underlying causes of the anger.

In the following example, Mike had been in hospital for two weeks preparing for a stem-cell transplant. Staff noticed that he had become increasingly bad-tempered and short with them. They had observed that he often became irritable after his wife had visited. Without realizing it, the nursing staff avoided unnecessary contact with him. One evening after his visitors had left and his medication was being dispensed Mike reacted angrily

Nurse: (enters room)

Mike: About time.

Nurse: Sorry we're a bit behind tonight. Supper was late getting up to us.

Mike: When's it ever on time?

Nurse: You sound fed up – do you want to talk about it now? (*empathy through reflection of feeling*)

Mike: No one seems to notice I'm in here half the time. I may as well not be here.

Nurse: What makes you think that? (*challenging beliefs and assumptions*)

Mike: Well, being stuck in here waiting for things to happen. I just feel so useless. No one tells me what's going on.

Nurse: It sounds like you feel a bit cut off from things. (*advanced empathy by picking out a theme*)

Mike: Well that's it; I am. At home I can see Jane's finding it hard with the kids, but she puts a brave face on it and won't really talk about it. Even in here, no one tells me what's happening.

Nurse: And that makes you feel . . .

Mike: It makes me feel angry and useless. Yeah and then I snap at you lot.

Nurse: Perhaps it's easier to be angry with supper being late than to talk to Jane about what's worrying you and how she's managing. (*drawing a conclusion and advanced empathy through making the implicit explicit*)

Here the nurse has picked up on and empathized with Mike's sense of being cut off. She has not been threatened by his show of emotion or become defensive, and has not tried to reassure him or suggest a remedy. Instead, she has helped Mike to see the link himself between feeling useless and being 'snappy' with the ward staff. It may now be appropriate to discuss what he might do about the situation.

Nurse: You said that you feel angry and useless at not being able to help Jane. Have you talked to her about how you're feeling?

Mike: No, there's no point.

Nurse: So Jane doesn't know how you're feeling just now? (*summarizing and drawing a conclusion*)

Mike: (shakes head)

Nurse: What do you think her reaction would be?

Mike: She'd probably say I'm being stupid and get upset.

Nurse: Is that the worst thing that could happen?' (*focusing and identifying assumptions*)

Mike: Yeah, I guess so. I don't want to upset her. She's got enough on her plate.

Nurse: So it's your fear of Jane becoming upset that is stopping you broaching the subject with her in the first place. Although you haven't really tested that out'. (*summarizing and drawing a conclusion*)

Mike: Yeah – but it's obvious she doesn't want to talk about problems at home.

Nurse: Why do you think that? (*assessing validity of his belief*)

Mike: She probably thinks it'll worry me.

Nurse: So the reason you don't ask her is for fear of upsetting her. And the reason she may not talk to you is because she doesn't want to worry you. (*summarizing*) Maybe you're both trying to protect each other rather than exclude one another. (*advanced empathy and suggestion of an alternative interpretation*)

Mike: That's true. I hadn't thought about it like that.

Nurse: Do you think it would be helpful to think about how you might talk to

Jane about what's worrying you? (*taking action through identifying the goal and problem solving*)

Mike: Maybe. We certainly can't go on like this.

Through listening and demonstrating a genuine concern to understand the sequence of his distress, the nurse was able to help Mike identify his key thoughts and feelings when his wife visited. By getting him to think through the worst consequence of talking to Jane, he was able to see that his anxious thoughts were unfounded. She also offered an alternative interpretation of what might be going on, that is, that they were both trying to protect one another, which he had not thought of before. In challenging the meaning Mike attributed to his wife's behaviour as well as his fears, the nurse was able to reach a point where he was open to explore options for change.

Aggression In a small minority of cases attempts to defuse a patient's anger do not succeed and they can become aggressive, exhibiting verbal and, in extreme cases, physical abuse. Often the only option open to help the person change is to confront them with the consequences of their behaviour and their model of the situation. This is the most direct form of challenging and should only be used when other strategies for change have failed.

Where a person's behaviour is causing you to feel threatened at any time, explain this and make clear the conditions under which you are willing to listen. Possible responses include:

'*I am happy to talk to you about this, but only if you stop shouting and calm down.*'

'*You are frightening me and other patients and I must ask you to calm down please.*'

'*If you do not stop shouting then I shall have to call security to remove you.*'

There will be occasions when the patient will wish to make a complaint. In such cases provide the appropriate information or provide a point of contact to the patient.

Guidelines for dealing with angry patients

- Keep calm. Allow the person to express their anger. Try not to take the person's anger personally.
- Speak slowly and quietly. Do not raise your voice as this can escalate the situation.

- Adopt an open and relaxed posture and maintain eye contact with the person.
- Do not be judgemental – rather reflect back what the patient's concerns are and how these are leaving them feeling (i.e. empathize). Acknowledge and reflect the feelings being expressed verbally and non-verbally.
- Try and see the situation from the patient's perspective.
- Refrain from offering your analysis of the situation too early, as this can seem judgemental and non-empathic and close down communication.
- Do not get into an argument about the factual content of what the person is saying before you have acknowledged their anger. Give information and correct misinformation after empathizing.
- Ask what would help them now and negotiate a solution. If this entails a person wishing to make a complaint, give them the information about how to proceed.
- If the patient is causing distress to other patients suggest moving to a private area.

The anxious patient

Anxiety is common in people with cancer and is a normal reaction to situations perceived as threatening. It becomes a problem when its symptoms interfere with a person's ability to cope with everyday life and their treatment. It can also be difficult for health care professionals to manage. We often respond to the manifestations of anxiety rather than its underlying causes. To manage a patient who is anxious the health professional needs to be able to recognize the triggers (or **a**ntecedents), symptoms (or **b**ehaviours) and **c**onsequences of their anxiety – the 'ABC' of anxiety management.

There are three components to anxiety and all are usually present, although the predominance and intensity of each will vary for each individual:

The cognitive component This includes worrying intrusive thoughts and beliefs about a situation. These thoughts are concerned with what *may* happen and typically focus on control, competence and acceptance.

> *'I'm bound to get side effects from chemotherapy and there's nothing I can do about it.'* (control)
> *'Will I be able to hold down my job?'* (competence)
> *'People will treat me differently.'* (acceptance)

The physiological component This includes physical symptoms such as nausea, sweating, diarrhoea, palpitations or increased heart rate, headaches, dizziness, dry mouth and trembling.

'I get butterflies in my stomach before my follow-up appointments.'
'I feel panicky.'
'I can't catch my breath.'

The behavioural component This includes irritability, forgetfulness, repeated checking, avoidance, and changes in eating and drinking habits.

'I always seem to be shouting at the kids these days.'
'I can't seem to stop eating.'
'I keep checking my body for signs that the cancer has come back.'

Many of the symptoms of anxiety mimic those of cancer and its treatments, making it difficult, at times, for patients to differentiate between the two. Moreover, the three components outlined above often interact with one other, giving rise to a vicious cycle. A good example of this is where somebody with cancer of the bowel mistakenly interprets anxiety-related diarrhoea as a manifestation of their disease.

In the following case study, Helen had been originally diagnosed with a malignant tumour in the thyroid. She initially appreciated her consultant's clear and straightforward explanation of what was wrong which gave her confidence in the care she was receiving. As she recalled:

'The consultant really seemed to know what she was talking about and it made absolute sense of what had been happening. She seemed to know her stuff.'

However, the diagnosis was subsequently reviewed and changed in the light of further investigations. Helen was treated with surgery and radiotherapy and appeared to have adjusted well to her treatment. At the end of her treatment, Helen began to worry about the reliability of the second diagnosis. She became preoccupied with her physical symptoms, in particular her chest pain, and repeatedly sought reassurance and confirmation of her diagnosis. The thought that the hospital might have made the wrong diagnosis kept coming to mind.

At first Helen's consultant either saw or spoke to her on the phone to reassure her. However, she became increasingly exasperated by Helen's repeated contact. She recognized that Helen was anxious but also realized that reassuring her was doing little to quell her anxiety. The consultant decided to raise the issue at their next meeting.

> *Doctor:* Hello, Helen. I'd like to discuss how you've been coping since we last met.
>
> *Helen:* OK, but I keep getting breathless and pains in my chest. I know you say there's nothing wrong but it worries me.
>
> *Doctor:* What do you think might be causing it? (*exploration of illness beliefs*)
>
> *Helen:* (cries) I know it's probably stupid but I really worry that it's something else serious.
>
> *Doctor:* Such as?
>
> *Helen:* I don't know really. I just keep thinking, oh it's come back, over and over again and that it's not been picked up. Then I get in a real panic and can't do anything.
>
> *Doctor:* So when you get these symptoms several things happen: you think that the cancer has come back; you worry that we've missed something – (*summarizing*) and it's that thought that makes you panic. (*tentative suggestion of alternative explanation*)
>
> *Helen:* Hmmm.
>
> *Doctor:* And what helps the panic?
>
> *Helen:* Well, speaking to you and trying to remember what you've said – that it's not the cancer coming back.
>
> *Doctor:* But the effect is short-lived; the thoughts come back and the cycle repeats itself. (*challenging unhelpful patterns of behaviour*)
>
> *Helen:* I know and I'm getting worse and you're probably fed up with me phoning.
>
> *Doctor:* Well, from what you say, phoning me isn't working long term – you carry on feeling anxious . . . (*challenging via reality checking and highlighting inconsistencies*)
>
> *Helen:* (cries)
>
> *Doctor:* . . . which is clearly upsetting you. What do you think about looking at what triggers your anxiety and panic and ways in which you can manage them? (*looking at options*)

When Helen began to talk about what had triggered her anxiety and re-peated contact several issues emerged. One was how vulnerable she felt now that her treatment and regular contact with the hospital team had come to an end. She was scared that the cancer might recur and found the uncertainty difficult to manage.

> *Helen:* 'At least when I was having my treatment it felt like I was doing some-thing about it. Now I wonder whether it's worked.'

Another issue was that her diagnosis and treatment had triggered a lot of unresolved issues surrounding her father's death ten years previously. He had been diagnosed with cancer of the stomach. There had been a delay in his referral to a specialist. For several months his GP had diagnosed and treated him for an ulcer. When he was eventually diagnosed, Helen's mother had insisted that no one in the family talk to him about the cancer. Helen felt guilty about this now, recalling that:

> *Helen:*   Despite being very close to my Dad and the one in the family to get things done, we all thought Mum's wishes were more important as she was his wife. So none of us talked to him about the cancer or really got involved in his treatment. I often think if I'd asked more questions maybe he would have got seen by the specialist quicker but I had a young family and had my hands full.

At this point her consultant sensed that a theme linking these various issues was uncertainty and how Helen dealt with that.

> *Doctor:*   You've identified several worries around for you at the moment – whether the cancer will recur; what your breathlessness and chest pain mean; have we got it right; whether you could have done more for your father (*summarizing*) – it strikes me that what they have in common is uncertainty. And it's this uncertainty that's making you feel anxious (*alternative interpretation*), a symptom of which can be breathlessness (*sharing information*), which in turn you're attributing to the cancer. (*identifying unhelpful thoughts*) And so a vicious cycle is created. (*challenging by presenting an alternative interpretation*)
>
> *Helen:*   Yes, but how do I stop it?
>
> *Doctor:*   I think it would be helpful to talk to someone who has expertise in anxiety management and who will be able to help you understand and deal with your anxiety better. What do you think about seeing the psychologist? (*advice and looking at options*)

Here the consultant has raised the possibility that Helen's anxiety is due to the uncertainty she is facing on different levels. In making this link she has demonstrated advanced empathy. This has opened the way for the consultant to suggest that Helen's breathlessness could be a result of anxiety. This has made some sense to Helen and allowed the consultant to get Helen to think about taking action to get specialist help to manage her anxiety.

The depressed patient

The management of depressed people entails helping them understand how their thoughts and feelings about an event can affect their behaviour. In promoting emotional well-being it is helpful for the health care professional to be familiar with the signs and symptoms of depression and comfortable in discussing these with the patient. The three principal components of depression are:

- behavioural
- cognitive
- physiological.

Behavioural Examples of the behavioural component include: withdrawal from enjoyable activities; indecisiveness; monotonous tone of voice; tearfulness; sighing; irritability; changes in eating habits (anorexia or bingeing); increased drug and alcohol consumption.

Cognitive Cognitions are the thoughts and beliefs experienced by individuals. This component typically includes: habitual negative thoughts; a difficulty in accessing positive thoughts; lowered concentration.

Physiological Physiological symptoms of depression include: loss of appetite; lowered libido; fatigue; sleep disturbance (including broken nights' sleep, early wakening or excessive sleeping); panic attacks.

When someone is depressed they can be difficult to engage. This can leave health care professionals feeling unsure how best to help. While depression is an understandable and common reaction for people facing cancer and its treatments, this does not mean that it should not be addressed and treated.

James, aged 35, had been diagnosed and treated for non-Hodgkin's lymphoma. He was happily married with two young children. He had been optimistic about his chemotherapy and was told he had a good prognosis. However, part way through his treatment it became clear that his cancer was not responding as hoped and it was stopped. Investigations revealed that his bone marrow had been affected and it was suggested that he start a different chemotherapy regime. He felt extremely tired and nauseous with the new treatment and complained of not being able to do anything. During a follow-up appointment he presented as very quiet and withdrawn and difficult to engage, which was a change from his previous demeanour.

Nurse: You seem very quiet today, James. Do you want to talk about it?

> *James:* Not really. Thanks for asking, but what's the point in talking? It's not going to change anything.
> *Nurse:* How do you mean? (*identifying beliefs*)
> *James:* Well, let's face it, my outlook doesn't look so good – and talking about it can't change that can it?
> *Nurse:* It may not effect how you respond to treatment but it could help you feel better in yourself. (*tackling unhelpful thoughts and assumptions*)

Here the nurse has picked up on James's change of behaviour and asked him about it. Rather than falsely reassuring him about his treatment, she has raised the possibility that talking about it could help him feel better. By doing so she has gently challenged his view that he can do nothing. It has also opened an avenue to explore and find out what his beliefs and feelings are about his future.

> *James:* If the chemo's going to work it'll work. Though I don't hold out much hope of it doing much.
> *Nurse:* What makes you think that? (*assessing validity of belief*)
> *James:* Well, the first lot didn't work and now my bones are affected, so it's a matter of time really. I'm not going to be cured – I'm palliative.
> *Nurse:* How do you see things panning out? (*focusing and exploration of beliefs*)
> *James:* Well, I'm going to die. I always thought that the cancer would get me, but hoped the chemotherapy would give me some more time. But I just seem to have come to a halt and don't have the energy to bounce back. I can't do anything, I feel sick, I don't enjoy anything any more and I don't see what would make it better.
> *Nurse:* What sort of things did you enjoy doing? (*tackling depressed thoughts by highlighting the positive exceptions*)
> *James:* Doing things with the children, spending time with friends – normal things.

In discussing James's depression, the nurse has been able to help him see how this further affects his own appraisal of his situation and what he can do to make himself feel better. By asking James to focus on what he enjoys, it is more likely that he will be able to generate some alternative coping strategies in future.

The patient who is suicidal

Although patients who are suicidal would seem to be rare, when cases arise they create considerable anxiety. Asking how a person sees the future is helpful in all cases and can enable any hopeless and suicidal thoughts to be logically explored.

Several years after surgery and treatment for cancer of the bowel Ros suffered a recurrence. She had adjusted well to her first treatment, but after this recent relapse complained of feeling totally hopeless and bleak about the future. Her doctor was aware that Ros had been feeling depressed and that she was taking anti-depressant medication prescribed by her GP.

Ros: I just can't seem to be bothered about anything really. My daughter is having a baby shortly and I can't get enthusiastic about it – which isn't like me – plus I'm crying all the time. I can't see any point to life and sometimes I think it would be better if I wasn't here.

Doctor: Do you ever feel like finishing it all? (*clarifying through closed question*)

Ros: Hmm. (nods and cries)

Doctor: How often do you feel like that? (*focusing*).

Ros: Quite often really.

Doctor: What – once a day or more than that?

Ros: I'd say more or less every day.

Doctor: Have you thought about what you might do? (*focusing via open question*)

Ros: I'd take all my tablets and go to sleep.

Doctor: How close have you got to doing that? (*focusing*)

Ros: Pretty close.

Doctor: How would you rate your risk of harming yourself – on a scale of 1 to 10? (*clarifying via reality check*)

Ros: When I get the thoughts about 7 or 8.

Doctor: So pretty high then. What stops you from taking the tablets? (*summarizing and highlighting a positive*)

Ros: I think how unfair it would be on my kids and my little grandchildren but then I think I'm no use to them the way I am anyway. (cries)

Doctor: Have you talked to anyone else about how you're feeling? (*focusing*)

Ros: (shakes head, cries)

Doctor: I can see it's very upsetting (*empathy via reflection of feeling*) and I'm glad you've been able to talk about it today. It's not easy. (*reinforcing the positive*)

Here the doctor has directly asked Ros about the presence, frequency and intensity of her suicidal thoughts. As the doctor has already established good rapport through the use of advanced empathy and encouragement, this direct line of questioning using closed questions has not appeared judgemental. Together they have been able to assess her risk of acting upon her thoughts. The doctor has been empathic and encouraging, which has helped Ros feel cared for rather than judged. He has positively reinforced her disclosure, acknowledging that it is difficult. This is important as people who feel suicidal often experience considerable guilt in disclosing it. The disclosure has opened the way for him to present her with an alternative view of what is going on and to flag his primary concern for her safety and the need for a specialist referral.

Doctor: When we're depressed it can cloud our view of things, leaving us feeling hopeless about being able to change anything and overwhelmed by it all. (*challenging via providing information and alternative interpretation*)

Ros: (cries)

Doctor: I think that it would be helpful to get advice as to how best to treat your depression and then see how things look to you. (*taking action by setting a goal*) What do you think about seeing someone? (*focusing*)

Ros: What – a shrink? You think I am mad, don't you? (laughs)

Doctor: No. I think you're very depressed (*confronts her model and presents his as an alternative*) and I think it would be helpful to see someone who is experienced in treating depression and who can help you. So I would like to refer you to a psychiatric colleague as a matter of some urgency and see you in a week's time for follow-up.

Ros: But what can they do?

Doctor: Well, that is part of what the person would discuss with you – ways that you can begin to feel better. (*providing information*) So, can we recap what we've agreed . . .

Here the doctor has directly confronted Ros's belief that she is mad and has given his alternative view that she is depressed. He has explained the reasoning behind his belief and recommended a referral to a specialist. He has done this in a way that is open and caring. When a patient does disclose suicidal thoughts, following guidelines, such as those below, can be helpful in assessing risk and reducing the health professional's anxiety.

Guidelines for dealing with patients who are suicidal

- Ask how a person sees the future, as a way of gauging the level of hopelessness.
- Ask whether they have or have had any suicidal thoughts.
- Ask about these suicidal thoughts, in particular their frequency, severity and persistence. Where there has been a previous suicide attempt ascertain how the person feels about it. If the person is upset at not having succeeded this is a cause for concern and needs to be discussed openly with the patient.

- Ask how much at risk of acting on these thoughts they feel now. Get them to rate their risk on a scale of 1 to 10.
- Ask about what prevents them from acting on their thoughts (for example family).
- Ask whether they have told anyone else how they have been feeling and find out what support or input from other agencies they have.
- Share the concerns about their safety that you have based on the above. Where patients do express suicidal ideas referral for psychological or psychiatric assessment should be discussed and arranged.
- Whether or not referral for psychological assessment is indicated, discuss and agree a plan of action that would help the person now and in the longer term. This might include: how to deal with any threat of self-harm while waiting to access specialist services; agreeing how the patient can make their environment safer, for example by telling someone at home about their suicidal thoughts and enlisting their help.
- Where it is felt that the person's safety is at immediate risk, liaise with the GP or psychiatric liaison services to seek further advice.
- Make a note of any agreed plans.

The demanding patient

Most health professionals will be able to think of patients who they experience as demanding. These patients can become very angry when the health professional fails to meet their requests, sometimes refusing to see a particular member of the care team. The responses they evoke vary, but commonly they include the health professional feeling criticized, irritated, stuck and at a loss about how to help.

Neil was 34 years old and had been diagnosed and treated for a melanoma. He had found the chemotherapy regime hard and had suffered severe nausea during much of the course of treatment. Shortly after the end of treatment he was admitted for investigation and treatment of a suspected recurrence. On the ward he frequently called staff, complaining of pain and requesting analgesic medication. He became angry when the staff did not respond immediately to his calls or were unable to increase his pain medication. Neil called the nurse.

Neil: Where's the doctor? I need something for this pain – it's not getting any better.

> *Nurse:* We have called him but he's dealing with another call at the moment.
> *Neil:* I need something now. Why can't you give me anything?
> *Nurse:* You're not due anything more for another couple of hours. The dose you're on should be sufficient to ease the pain. You'll just have to wait, I'm afraid, until the registrar comes.
> *Neil:* You obviously don't appreciate what I'm going through. I want to speak to someone who can do something now.
> *Nurse:* I've already explained that the registrar is on his way. Now I am really busy; we're just about to do the handover, so please be patient.

Here the nurse has reacted to the patient in a defensive way. At no time does she ask about the pain or what the patient could do until the doctor arrives. This has had the effect of making Neil feel dismissed.

In the next scenario the nurse approaches Neil to talk about his pain and repeated calling of the nursing staff.

> *Nurse:* I'd like to talk to you about what's been going on and how you're managing your pain.
> *Neil:* I've told you what will help and that's the one thing you say you can't give me.
> *Nurse:* I realize you're in pain and that it must be frustrating to have to wait for the Doctor. (*empathizes via reflection of feeling*) We are all concerned to get your pain under control. But I'm afraid only the doctor can authorize any stronger medication. He knows the situation and is on his way but is likely to be another half an hour. (*providing information*) Until then is there anything that would help you with the pain? (*action via looking forward*)
> *Neil:* Like what?
> *Nurse:* Well, have you noticed anything that helps ease the pain? (*focusing*)
> *Neil:* I know what makes it worse – getting wound up waiting for some doctor to get here.
> *Nurse:* So feeling wound up makes it worse? Have you noticed what helps?
> *Neil:* Listening to the radio helps take my mind off it but it's still there.
> *Nurse:* How is it now?
> *Neil:* A bit better.
> *Nurse:* So distracting yourself from the pain, whilst not taking it away, helps a bit? (*summarizes*)
> *Neil:* Yeah, I guess so.
> *Nurse:* We are just going into handover so I'm going to have to go. I will pass on what's happening. How about trying to listen to the radio and see if that helps? (*action by setting a goal*) I'll pop back to see you before I go off.

Here the nurse has proactively explained what the position is regarding the doctor and has challenged his notion that no one cares. She has brought the focus onto what might help Neil manage while waiting. In doing so she has given the message that he has a role to play in the management of his pain. Together they have identified that distraction helps. Finally the nurse has explained that she cannot make more time now, but has agreed to come back after the handover and to update the rest of the team on his situation.

In summary, demanding patients can often leave the health professional feeling inadequate and unable to get things right. It is particularly helpful to be honest and realistic with such patients and to encourage them to identify things they can do to help contain their sense of frustration appropriately.

Multiple losses and previous trauma

In addition to the losses arising from the cancer itself, previous losses and traumas can often be reignited. These need to be considered as they can affect a patient's adjustment, as illustrated in the following case study:

Harry was a 51-year-old taxi driver. He was diagnosed with a brain tumour after he had collapsed in the street. Together, the tumour and necessary surgery had left him with some cognitive impairment. Of particular concern to Harry's wife was his unsteadiness on his feet and forgetfulness. For Harry the major concerns were his driving licence being withdrawn and not being able to provide for his family and 'getting upset all the time'. His one pleasure was gardening. However, his wife did not like to leave him alone for any period of time for fear that he would collapse as before. This caused tension and arguments between them, with Harry seeing his wife's behavior as taking away his one area of enjoyment and independence.

Prior to his collapse and diagnosis he had been fiercely independent and described himself as 'always being there for other people'. He was the eldest child of five in his family and had always been the responsible one. In talking to him the doctor wondered whether there was something about Harry's need to provide for and support his family that was preventing him from accepting his wife's attempts to look after him.

Doctor: It seems difficult to think that your wife is worried about you. (*advanced empathy through making the implicit explicit*)
Harry: Maybe.

> *Doctor:* What makes it so difficult? (*assessing validity of assumption*)
> *Harry:* All my life, I've been the one who's sorted out everyone else's problems and given them support. But I can't do that any more. Since my illness I can't drive, I can't work – I can't even do a bit of gardening without the wife on at me.
> *Doctor:* So in the past you've been the one to support others. I wonder whether it's that which is making it so hard to let others support and do things for you now? (*advanced empathy by identifying a theme*)

At this point Harry began to sob uncontrollably. The sense of loss at not being able to support his family was clearly upsetting. However, the doctor sensed it was triggering other distressing feelings in Harry. To check out his hunch he asked:

> *Doctor:* It's obviously very upsetting to talk about these things. (*empathy via reflection of feeling*) Can you remember a time when you've felt like this before in your life? (*exploring triggers*)

It transpired that Harry's younger brother had been killed in a playground accident when in his charge. This had a devastating effect on him and his family. His parents blamed him and in turn he blamed himself. He clearly recalled thinking that nothing he could ever do would help lessen the pain of his brother's death, which remained overwhelmingly upsetting for him. At the time no one stopped to consider his feelings and the death was never talked about. As a result Harry tried to make things better by providing for and looking after his family.

When his feelings surrounding his brother's death were explored, he was able to see that he had never allowed himself to mourn the loss of his brother. Instead he reacted by internalizing his feelings and directing his attention to providing for his family in an attempt to compensate for what had happened. In identifying the recurring theme of loss in his life and exploring his reaction to it, Harry was able to see how his difficulties in accepting help now were intertwined with his unresolved feelings over his brother's death. This realization helped him to reappraise what had happened and gave him and his wife an inroad into understanding and making sense of his current distress. He was able to articulate a core belief that his brother's death was his fault. At this point the doctor was able to suggest that Harry's guilt over his brother's death was what was making it so hard for him to accept help and concern from other people.

> *Doctor:* It's as if you still can't accept help for yourself because of what hap-
> pened to your brother? (*advanced empathy by making the implicit explicit*)

In checking out his hunch the doctor had been able to help Harry realize how
the unresolved loss of his brother's death was impeding his own adjustment to
the losses he was now facing.

At this point his wife talked to him about the other alternative explanations
for his brother's death. This was the first time that they had talked about his
brother's death and its impact on him. It was clearly very emotional for both
of them and they wept openly. At the end of the meeting, Harry and his wife
were better able to understand why he was finding it so hard to adapt to his
loss of ability and why he got cross when she tried to care for him.

Bringing the meeting to a close the doctor asked:

> *Doctor:* What would help you most now in dealing with your present situation?
> (*action via looking forward*)

From here they were able to identify two main issues and goals: to negotiate
a compromise regarding Harry's gardening and for Harry to talk about his
brother's death. The referral on for more specialist counselling and support
was also discussed.

The following guidelines may be useful in managing multiple-loss situations:

Guidlines for dealing with multiple losses
- Acknowledge various changes and losses that the cancer has and the
  thoughts and feelings associated with these.
- Ask about previous losses and bereavements and the effect that the person's cancer has had on these.
- Ask what role the person typically played in their family at times of loss
  and change.
- Discuss what the losses mean for the person. Specifically identify core
  beliefs and thoughts about loss and the consequences these have for the
  person regarding feelings and behaviour.

Conclusion

In this chapter we have looked at situations regarded as difficult by health
professionals. Where adaptation and change become difficult for patients, the

use of challenging skills can be very helpful in enabling them to see how their thoughts and beliefs are linked to their feelings and behaviour. The key task for the health professional is to elicit a patient's thoughts and beliefs about their situation and question the basis and usefulness of these. It is then possible to help them to consider alternative ways of thinking and behaving and, by testing the validity of their assumptions, enable a reappraisal of their view of the world.

There will be times when you will feel unable to manage particular situations or help a patient resolve their distress. When this happens it is best to be honest with the patient and discuss other sources of help.

Summary

- People often resist change and as a result difficulties can occur for both the patient and the health professional, particularly when feelings and concerns are not expressed.
- Situations described by health care professionals as difficult include dealing with patients who are distressed, angry, anxious, depressed, suicidal or facing multiple losses.
- The first step in managing difficult situations is to acknowledge that there is a problem, so as to focus attention on it rather than labelling the patient as difficult.
- In addition to basic (level 1) counselling skills, it is sometimes appropriate to use higher-level challenging skills. These encourage patients to re-evaluate their model of the world and formulate new ways of managing their illness.
- While each situation may call for a different approach, there are some general guidelines that can assist in managing difficult situations.
- In using challenging skills, it is important to remember that how things are said, rather than what is said, often determines a successful outcome. Refrain from offering an analysis of the situation too early, as this can seem judgemental, non-empathic and a barrier to communication. Challenging is most successful where a good rapport has been established.
- Try to observe any triggers (**A**ntecedents), symptoms (**B**ehaviours) and discuss these and their **C**onsequences with the patient – the so-called ABC approach.

- Challenging beliefs and assumptions can be helpful in enabling a patient to review their appraisal of their world. It can also assist them to question and test out the validity of their assumptions.
- Health care professionals need to be aware of their own reactions and feelings towards the patient and the situations they face and attempt to keep them separate.
- It is helpful to identify and clarify a person's feelings before challenging them. Simply eliciting and containing a person's distress can be beneficial in helping them to adjust. Ask patients what would help their situation and focus on what they could do to make it better; be open and honest and be prepared to explain the reasons behind your thinking and advice.
- Picking out themes can be helpful in enabling people to make links between different issues and ultimately to understand how their beliefs about their world affect their ability to adjust to aspects of their illness.
- Carers need to recognize when the use of challenging skills is appropriate, and whether they possess adequate experience or should refer on to a more experienced practitioner or specialist.

Chapter Eight

Professional Issues in Cancer Care

By now we hope to have demonstrated the central importance of good communication in the care and well-being of people with cancer. So far, we have described and illustrated the skills that underpin clear communication throughout the various stages of a person's cancer journey. This chapter will examine some of the organizational and individual barriers to the use of communication and counselling skills. It will then look at the psychological impact on helpers of caring for people with cancer and propose some mechanisms to ameliorate this. The need for training, supervision and support for staff in developing and maintaining these skills will be considered as well as the importance of maintaining the emotional well-being of cancer clinicians.

Barriers to Communication and Counselling in the NHS

Despite the clinically proven benefits of including psychosocial factors in the management of patients with cancer and the expectation that effective communication is part of the duties of health professionals, a number of major organizational issues act as barriers to change.

Organizational barriers

Regardless of the skill and motivation of an individual practitioner, barriers within his or her organization can be insurmountable and so result in the deterioration of skills and increasing hopelessness. Pressure on time and lack of private space – may be a reflection of what is perhaps the biggest organizational obstacle of all. Effective communication is less valued than other more technical aspects of health care. This affects the quality of service provided to patients, particularly where staff support structures are weak. In these cases, there is evidence that health care professionals use distancing tactics when dealing with patients (Wilkinson, 1991).

Time One of the major obstacles is time. With difficulties in recruitment and retention of staff and pressure to treat people within tighter time-frames, the perception of lack of available time is increasing. There is a corresponding belief that effective communication requires more time than standard practice allows and does not offer good value for money.

To counter these arguments, communication lies at the heart of every clinical interaction. Moreover, there is a large body of research evidence showing that good communication skills lead to increased patient satisfaction, fewer complaints and increased compliance with treatment programmes. These are increasingly recognized as service-quality measures.

Effective communication yields improvements even in basic history taking, which in turn can have a significant impact upon clinical decision making. In addition, many patients present again if a significant concern has not been addressed in the initial consultation – a clear case for seeing effective communication as a valuable resource, worthy of investment.

Physical environment In a practical sense, the physical environment in many hospitals does not allow for the basic requirements of effective communication. This may be particularly so in the ward setting, where there is limited access to private space and staff have a number of demands upon them at any one time.

Continuity of care A final consideration is the lack of continuity in care, and this can make it difficult to develop a meaningful relationship with a patient. The development of cancer networks may enable local groups of staff involved in the care of patients with cancer to agree on protocols for the routine provision of information and support. The individual ways of interacting with patients that we have been discussing in the previous chapters can be further improved by taking a service-level view on information and support, rather than devolving the decision entirely to individual clinicians. Differences between health professionals in the way they handle these issues can be confusing to the patient. Inadequately written notes can leave other professionals unclear about the messages previously given, meaning that patients do not receive consistent management. In the worst case, this can reduce the trust of the patient, who may, at a time of high anxiety, perceive the differences to be indicative of incompetence.

Individual barriers

Good basic communication skills should be used by any health professional regardless of their view of their role in health care. In reality, health professionals often find them difficult to put into practice. At the most basic level, some do not realize that spending time talking to patients can have a material impact on clinical outcome. This may be a hangover from earlier, more paternalistic, models of the doctor–patient relationship, where patients were seen as grateful and passive recipients of health care. Thus a patient given advice by a health professional was expected to follow it without question; there was no need for discussion and negotiation about what they had been told.

This 'expert' model is giving way to more collaborative approaches, with health care being seen as a partnership. In this new relationship the health professional views patients in a broader context and as having the right to consent to the services provided for them. Equally, the patient is more likely to see the health professional as an agent to improve their health by directly offering investigations and intervention, but also by helping them to tackle the problems associated with ill-health. Developing the confidence to apply communication and counselling skills within a collaborative relationship may require health professionals to challenge their own beliefs about the role of the patient so that they feel comfortable sharing responsibility for the patient's health.

Similarly, there is a fear that starting a conversation with a patient about a difficult subject may open a Pandora's box of problems that could overwhelm both parties. There is the implication that the situation could get out of control and might irrevocably damage both individuals. Concerns of this sort can inhibit people from even attempting to change how they interact with patients, and so prevent them from discovering that their predictions are largely unfounded. It is unrealistic to think that difficult issues can be side-stepped; they have a habit of presenting themselves anyway, whether health professionals feel they have the skills to deal with them or not.

Finally, communication skills may be seen as somehow different from any other skills in the health professional's toolkit. They can be seen as mysterious or as something that you are either born with or not. People might be construed as good or bad communicators, with those who are lacking in the skills being unable to be trained to develop them. Again this perception can prevent staff learning about or using communication skills. It can also prevent health service managers from investing in the necessary training resources. There is, however, clear evidence in many areas of work that these skills can be taught and learnt. Although some people may be more naturally inclined towards developing them, most people can improve their competency, with benefits for all.

The Psychological Impact of Caring for People with Cancer

There is no doubt that caring for people with serious diseases such as cancer has the potential to be a stressful experience. It is possible, over time, to become burnt out by the day-to-day care of others (Maslach 1981). This might manifest itself as emotional numbness and an increasing difficulty in empathizing with one's patients. Part of offering a psychological perspective on services is to consider the effect of the work on health care professionals, and how their thoughts and feelings about their work can influence how it is delivered.

Studies of doctors working in a range of settings in the UK have shown a significant amount of anxiety and depression (Caplan 1994). Of senior non-surgical cancer doctors, very nearly a third were reported to have probable psychiatric morbidity using the General Health Questionnaire (GHQ), with clinical oncologists faring worse (Ramirez et al. 1995). Higher levels of distress were associated with feeling overloaded, dealing with treatment toxicity or error and deriving little satisfaction from professional status or esteem. Those who felt insufficiently trained in communication and management skills reported higher levels of distress. In addition, stress from work taking a toll on home life has also been associated with both burnout and psychiatric morbidity (Ramirez et al. 1996).

The motivations of those joining health professions, such as wanting to help or cure others, can generate high expectations which may be unrealistic, particularly in cancer care. Health care professionals need to accept that, in many cases, patients are not going to get better, and that some of the treatments leading to cure can be very distressing.

Perhaps of most relevance in the context of a discussion about communication, the above factors were also associated with low satisfaction with relationships with patients, relatives and other staff (Ramirez et al. 1996). This final observation suggests that improved communication skills may indeed be of psychological benefit to staff as well as to patients (Davis and Fallowfield 1991).

Given these significant levels of distress among health professionals, dealing with one's own distressing emotional reactions might be an important area of personal development.

Supporting Effective Communication in the Workplace

In order to promote effective communication in health settings, changes seem to be required at a number of levels.

Managerial support

Support from managers in particular may be considered as providing the foundation on which the development and use of individuals' skills can be built. This may be demonstrated in the adoption of guidelines for providing information and support to patients, or be reflected in revised mission statements or policies that stress the need to take care over communication with patients and colleagues. This is beginning to be reflected at a national level, for example by the provision of guidelines on psychosocial support for women with breast cancer in Australia backed up with funding to help the transmission of communication skills. In the United Kingdom the NHS Cancer Plan stated:

> By 2002 it will be a pre-condition of qualification to deliver patient care in the NHS that staff are able to demonstrate competence in communication with patients. And for cancer we shall give staff additional training in communication skills, and in the provision of psychological support. We will ensure that high quality written or other forms of information are available.

Environment

An element of reorganization of the work setting is also required, for example ensuring the availability of private rooms for bad-news interviews. Equally, the planning of services would benefit from some restructuring, allowing professionals adequate time to conduct particularly sensitive interviews at particular points in the cancer journey. Some general practitioners, for example, have been proactive in arranging longer appointments in anticipation of the distress of a newly diagnosed patient as an investment in the continuing relationship that will be required to see them through the events that follow.

Co-ordination and integration of services

The use of relevant resources in the local area, for example information and support services in cancer centres or mental health services, or more experienced colleagues or peers, is invaluable in providing a network of support which can help to underpin a more collaborative relationship with patients. They can offer advice about sources of helpful information and practical support, for example financial assistance to help with travel costs from some of the cancer charities. Additionally, they may be able to assist in the development of policies and guidance for professionals on the effective provision of information and support. Mental health specialists in particular can offer help with understanding patients' reactions and dealing with difficult communication issues. In addition, they can offer assessment and specialist interventions for those who are particularly distressed.

Training

Individual health professionals may need to examine and challenge their own beliefs regarding the use of communication skills. This may include their perceptions of the usefulness of the skills, the possibility of learning these skills, and competence in using them effectively.

Formal training, both pre- and post-qualification, is related to improvements in communication. This is increasingly recognized in the undergraduate training of most health professionals. There is still a great need for post-qualification training. Some of the cancer charities, for example the Cancer Research Campaign, have supported the development of evidence-based training programmes in communication skills for cancer professionals (Parle et al. 1997).

Effective training programmes should:

- provide information about the characteristics and benefits of good communication, as well as about the health professional behaviours that deter the patient from expressing concerns;
- provide information about the psychological difficulties of cancer patients;
- explore and challenge beliefs that would interfere with adopting new communication behaviours, for example that it would take too long, or is not a legitimate part of the professional's role;
- provide micro-skills training, with an emphasis on developing a perception of competency among participants through modelling and positively reinforcing attempts to modify behaviour in role play;
- develop goals and implementation plans to enhance transfer of skills to the workplace, including eliciting support from managers and accessing personal support and supervision, and offer follow-up.

Ongoing access to training to update and revise skills is an important element of maintaining good practice.

Support and supervision

Equally, supervision can be a useful tool to promote continued practice, as well as allowing health professionals to discuss their concerns and learn to work within their personal limitations. Ideally, supervisors should be familiar with psycho-oncology but not be the professional's manager. They should be familiar with the communication skills found to be effective with cancer patients and able to provide encouragement and constructive feedback about their application. As with therapeutic relationships, the supervisor should be able to develop a rapport with the professional, demonstrating respect and genuine interest in their professional development. Discussion of cases, or even reviewing tape-recordings of interviews, can help to increase awareness of the skills being used and of any blocks to good communication that require attention. Suitable supervisors may be found among the local network of health services. These might include, for example, clinical psychologists working in oncology.

Given the potential for distress among cancer professionals, access to supervision may also help the person being supervised to develop personal resources to manage the stress of this area of work. These might include exploring and challenging salient beliefs about personal responsibility for patients' distress and the need to attend to self-care strategies such as taking breaks. Improving satisfaction with professional relationships and developing skills in maintaining one's own emotional health contribute to a healthy and effective work-force.

Improved teamworking

Conflict with other health professionals can contribute to the stress of individual members of staff, whereas a supportive team can help to protect them from other sources of stress. Improved communication skills, particularly those of active listening, can be put to good use within a team. They are likely to have a beneficial impact upon teamworking, helping to create the sort of work environment which will be perceived by staff as supportive. In a time of difficulty with recruiting and retaining specialist staff this may have the additional affect of reducing staffing problems generally.

Specialist support

Access to effective employee assistance facilities, such as confidential counselling, is considered a prerequisite of good human resources management in many fields of work. Some health settings already provide access to these resources, and health professionals and managers should be encouraged to develop a healthy attitude towards their use in proactive stress management and to recognize the need to tackle levels of stress which may threaten good patient care. There are undoubtedly reservations amongst staff groups about the use of such services, and so their provision needs to be carefully thought through and promoted sensitively in the workplace to ensure optimal use.

Conclusion

This book was written for all health professionals working with cancer patients, with two main aims in mind: firstly, to provide an understanding of the psychological issues involved in caring for those affected by cancer, and of how health professionals may influence their adjustment to the disease; secondly, to explain and illustrate how health professionals can learn and use communication and counselling skills to promote well-being in those affected by cancer.

In addition to the physical aspects of their disease, patients with cancer face major psychosocial issues. These vary according to the individual and the stage of their cancer journey. By listening and talking to patients, health professionals play an important role in helping them make the many psychological adjustments that will be required along the way.

We hope that the book will give you a fuller understanding of the patient's experience of cancer, and help you to play an effective part in assisting them at a difficult time. We also hope that you will feel more confident to discuss issues with patients, and that you will seek out support from trainers and supervisors to help you develop your skills further.

Health professionals and patients can all benefit from more attention being paid to the communication issues described in this book. We thank you for reading it and wish you the best of luck in implementing the skills.

Summary

- Effective communication is an essential element of all health professionals' duties.

- There are major organizational obstacles to be overcome in order to optimize the development and use of communication skills. These include the belief that 'talking' would be better provided by specialists such as counsellors, time pressure, lack of continuity of care making it hard to develop relationships with patients, and the lack of private space.

- In addition, there are few professional groups who see it as their responsibility to champion the need for funding and support for the development and use of communication and counselling skills.

- Health professionals may be unsure about how to offer a more collaborative partnership style of relationship with their patients, or fear opening a Pandora's box of problems which they are not able to contain.

- Communication and counselling skills can be seen as something you cannot be trained in, and so the need for training and support goes unrecognized.

- There are significant psychological consequences for staff in caring for patients with cancer, including burnout and psychiatric morbidity, which are more likely in those dissatisfied with their relationships with patients, relatives and other staff.

- Effective communication requires some organizational changes, including in the physical environment and in raising the respect in which these skills are held. This requirement is now reflected in the NHS Cancer Plan.

- Individual professionals may need to identify and weigh up any misgivings they have about incorporating some of the ideas discussed in this book.

- They may also need to embark upon further effective training; models such as that developed by the Cancer Research Campaign are providing a benchmark.

- Local mental health resources should be identified to support the work of cancer health professionals, as sources of advice and specialist assessment and treatment.

- Supervision can be sought from a suitably qualified professional to help generalize communication skills learned on courses or through other means.

- Improved teamwork may be a consequence of the use of communication and counselling skills, and this may have a beneficial effect on staff recruitment and retention.
- Access to effective employee assistance services, such as counselling, may need to be introduced where it is not already available, and their use promoted within the workplace.

Bibliography

Anderson, E. A. (1987). Preoperative preparation for cardiac surgery facilitates recovery, reduces psychological distress, and reduces the influence of acute postoperative hypertension. *Journal of Consulting and Clinical Psychology*, 55, 513–20.

Baumann L. J., Cameron, L. D., Zimmerman, R. S. and Leventhal, H. (1989). Illness representations and matching labels with symptoms. *Health Psychology*, 8, 449–69.

British Association of Counselling Code of Ethics and Practice for Counsellors (regularly updated and available at www.bac.co.uk).

Brown, G. W. and Harris, T. (1978). *Social Origins of Depression: A Study of Psychiatric Disorder in Women*. Cambridge: Cambridge University Press.

Burgess, C. C., Ramirez, A. J., Richards, M. A. and Love, S. B. (1998). Who and what influences delayed presentation in breast cancer? *British Journal of Breast Cancer*, 77, 1343–8.

Burton, M. and Watson, M. (1998). *Counselling People with Cancer*. Chichester: Wiley.

Cancer Research Campaign (1998 and general). See resources section or visit www.crc.org.uk.

Caplan, R. P. (1994). Stress, anxiety, and depression in hospital consultants, general practitioners, and senior health service managers. *British Medical Journal*, 309, 1261–3.

Davis, H. and Fallowfield, L. (1991). Evaluating the effects of counselling and communication, in Davis, H. and Fallowfield, L. (eds), *Counselling and Communication in Healthcare*. Chichester: Wiley.

Department of Health (2001). *The NHS Cancer Plan: A Plan for Investment, A Plan for Reform*. © Crown copyright.

Derogatis, L. R., Morrow, G., Fettig, J., Penman, D., Piasetsky, S., Schmale, A. M., Henrichs, M. and Carnicke, C. L. (1983). The prevalence of psychiatric disorders among cancer patients. *Journal of the American Medical Association*, 249, 751–7.

Devlen, J., Maguire, P., Phillips, P., Crowther, D. and Chambers, H. (1987). Psychological problems associated with diagnosis and treatment of lymphomas II: A prospective study. *British Medical Journal*, 295, 956–7.

Diamond, J. (1998). *C Because Cowards get Cancer too* . . . London: Vermilion.

Egan, G. (1998). *The Skilled Helper Model: Skills and Methods for Efffective Helping*, 6th edn. Monterey, CA: Brooks/Cole.

Egbert, L. D., Battit, G. E., Welch, C. E. and Bartlett, M. K. (1964). Reduction of postoperative pain by encouragement and instruction of patients. *New England Journal of Medicine*, 270, 825–7.

Fallowfield, L. J., Hall, A., Maguire, G. P. and Baum, M. J. (1990). Psychological outcomes of different treatment policies in women with early breast cancer. *British Medical Journal*, 301, 575–80.

Faulkner, A. and Maguire, P. (1994). *Talking to Cancer Patients and their Relatives*. Oxford: Oxford University Press.

Folkman, S. and Greer, S. (2000). Promoting psychological well-being in the face of serious illness: when theory, research and practice inform each other. *Psycho-oncology*, 9, 11–19.

Greer, S., Morris, T. and Petingale, K. W. (1979). Psychological responses to breast cancer: effect on outcome. *Lancet*, ii, 785–7.

Hughes, J. (1985). Depressive illness and lung cancer: 11. Follow-up of inoperable patients. *European Journal of Surgical Oncology*, 11, 21–4.

Hughson, A., Cooper, A., McArdle, C. and Smith, D. (1986). Psychological impact of adjuvant chemotherapy in the first two years after mastectomy. *British Medical Journal*, 293, 1268–72.

Hughson, A., Cooper, A., McArdle, C. and Smith, D. (1987). Psychosocial effects of radiotherapy after mastectomy. *British Medical Journal*, 294, 1515–16.

Kiebert, G., de Haes, J. and Van de Velde, C. (1991). The impact of breast conserving treatment and mastectomy on the quality of life of early stage breast cancer patients: a review. *Journal of Clinical Oncology*, 9, 1059–70.

King, K. B., Nail, L. M., Kreamer, K., Stroll, R. A. and Johnson, J. E. (1985). Patients' descriptions of the experience of receiving radiation therapy. *Oncology Nursing Forum*, 12, 55–61.

Lazarus, R. S. and Folkman, S. (1984). *Stress, Appraisal and Coping*. New York: Springer.

Lee, M., Love, S., Mitchell, J., Parker, E., Rubens, R., Watson, J., Fentiman, I. and Hayward, J. (1992). Mastectomy or conservation for early breast cancer: psychological morbidity. *European Journal of Cancer*, 26A, 1340–4.

Leventhal, H., Meyer, D. and Nerenz, D. (1980). The common sense representation of illness danger, in Rachman, S. (ed.), *Contribution to Medical Psychology: Vol. 2*, 7–30. New York: Pergamon Press.

Leventhal, H., Nerenz, D. R. and Steele, D. J. (1984). Illness representations and coping with health threats, in Baum, A., Taylor, S. E. and Singer, J. E. (eds) *Handbook of Psychology and Health: Vol. 4*, 219–52. Hillsdale, NJ: Lawrence Erlbaum Associates.

Ley, P. (1982). Giving information to patients, in Eiser, J. R. (ed.) *Social Psychology and Behavioural Medicine*. Chichester: Wiley.

Maguire, P. (1984). Communication and patient care, in Steptoe, A. and Matthews, A. (eds), *Health and Human Behaviour*, 153–73. London: Academic Press.

Maguire, P. (1985). Towards more effective psychological intervention in patients with cancer. *Cancer Care*, 2, 12–15.

Maguire, P. (1989). Breast conservation vs. mastectomy: psychological considerations. *Seminars in Surgical Oncology*, 5, 137–44.

Maslach, C. (1981). *Burn Out: The Cost of Caring*. Englewood Cliffs, NJ: Prentice-Hall.

Morris, J. and Royle, G. T. (1988). Offering patients a choice of surgery for early breast cancer: a reduction in anxiety and depression in patients and their husbands. *Social Science and Medicine*, 26, 583–5.

Morrow, G. R. (1982). Prevalence and correlates of anticipatory nausea and vomiting in chemotherapy patients. *Journal of the National Cancer Institute*, 68, 585–8.

Nichols, K. (1984). *Psychological Care in Physical Illness*. Beckenham: Croom Helm.

Parle, M., Jones, B. and Maguire, P. (1994). Coping with multiple demands of cancer: patients' appraisal patterns, coping responses and mental health [Abstract]. *Psycho-oncology*, 3, 149.

Parle, M., Maguire, P. and Heaven, C. (1997). The development of a training model to improve health professionals' skills, self-efficacy, and outcome expectations when communicating with cancer. *Social Science and Medicine*, 44, 231–40.

Peck, A. and Boland, J. (1977). Emotional reactions to radiation treatment. *Cancer*, 40, 180–4.

Pinder, K. L., Ramirez, A. J., Richards, M. A. and Gregory, W. M. (1994). Cognitive responses and psychiatric disorder in women with operable breast cancer. *Psycho-oncology*, 3, 129–37.

Ramirez, A. J., Graham, J., Richards, M. A., Cull, A. and Gregory, W. M. (1996). Mental health of hospital consultants: the effects of stress and satisfaction at work. *Lancet*, 347, 724–8.

Ramirez, A. J., Graham, J., Richards, M. A., Cull, A., Gregory, W. M., Leaning, M. S., Snashall, D. C. and Timothy, A. R. (1995). Burnout and psychiatric disorder among cancer clinicians. *British Journal of Cancer*, 71, 1263–9.

Ramirez, A. J., Richards, M. A., Jarrett, S. R. and Fentiman, I. S. (1995). Can mood disorder in women with breast cancer be identified preoperatively? *British Journal of Cancer*, 72, 1509–12.

Ramirez, A. J., Westcombe, A. M., Burgess, C. C., Sutton, S., Littlejohns, P. and Richards, M. A. (1999). Factors predicting delayed presentation of symptomatic breast cancer: a systematic review. *Lancet*, 353, 1127–31.

Ridgeway, V. and Mathews, A. (1982). Psychological preparation for surgery: a comparison of methods. *British Journal of Clinical Psychology*, 21, 271–80.

Rogers, C. R. (1957). The necessary and sufficient conditions of therapeutic personality change. *Journal of Consulting Psychology*, 21, 154–61.

Sellick, S. M. and Crooks, D. L. (1999). Depression and cancer: an appraisal of the literature for prevalence, detection and practice guideline development for psychological interventions. *Psycho-oncology*, 8, 315–33.

Seyrek, S. K., Corah, N. L. and Pace, L. F. (1984). Comparison of three distraction techniques in reducing stress in dental patients. *Journal of the American Dental Associa-*

tion, 108, 327–9.

Speigel, D. (1985). Psychosocial intervention with cancer patients. *Journal of Psychosocial Oncology*, 3, 83–95.

Suls, J. and Wan, C. K. (1989). Effects of sensory and procedural information on coping with stressful medical procedures and pain: a meta-analysis. *Journal of Consultant Clinical Psychology*, 57, 372–9.

Wardle, F. J., Collins, W., Pernet, A. L., Whitehead, M. I., Bourne, T. H. and Campbell, S. (1993). Psychological impact of screening for familial ovarian cancer. *Journal of the National Cancer Institute*, 85, 653–7.

Watson, M., Greer, S., Blake, S. and Shrapnell, K. (1984). Reaction to a diagnosis of breast cancer: relationship between denial, delay and rates of psychological morbidity. *Cancer*, 53, 2008–12.

Watson, M., Law, M., dos Santos, M., Greer, S., Baruch, J. and Bliss, J. (1994). The Mini-MAC: further development of the Mental Adjustment to Cancer Scale. *Journal of Psychosocial Oncology*, 12, 33–46.

Weisman, A. D. and Worden, J. W. (1976–7). The existential plight in cancer: significance of the first 100 days. *International Journal of Psychiatric Medicine*, 7, 1–15.

Wells, J. K., Howard, G. S., Nowlin, W. F. and Vargas, M. J. (1986). Presurgical anxiety and postsurgical pain and adjustment: effects of a stress inoculation procedure. *Journal of Consulting and Clinical Psychology*, 54, 831–5.

Wilkinson, S. (1991). Factors which influence how nurses communicate with cancer patients. *Journal of Advanced Nursing*, 16, 677–88.

Resources

General Sources of Information

The Cancer Research Campaign offers thorough and reliable information for health professionals and patients on its website at www.crc.org.uk, including statistics on the incidence of cancer and links to their dedicated patient information site Cancerhelp UK (www.cancerhelp.org.uk).

CancerBACUP provides well-researched information about cancer for patients and health professionals through its website at www.cancerbacup.org.uk.

Cancerlink provide an excellent guide to cancer services through their Directory of Cancer Support and Self-help which is available from: Cancerlink, 11–21 Northdown Street, London N1 9BN or telephone 020 7833 2818.

Information about Cancer Trials

www.cto.mrc.ac.uk provides information from the Medical Research Council's Clinical Trials Unit, with information for patients about the nature of clinical trials and considerations about joining one.

Training Resources

CRC Psychological Medicine Group provide training in communication skills that have been well documented and researched. They can be contacted at the Christie Hospital, Wilmslow Road, Withington, Manchester M20 4BX or by telephone on 0161 446 3688 or 3681.

Specialist training courses in the use of cognitive behavioural therapy are also available; further details are available from the Psychological Medicine

Department at the Royal Marsden Hospital, Downs Road, Sutton, Surrey, SM2 5PT, tel. 020 8642 6011, fax 020 8643 2621.

Information about Psychosocial Support

If you wish to refer a patient for additional assistance with dealing with the emotional effects of cancer, you can contact the following organizations:

- British Psychological Society (www.bps.org.uk)
- British Association for Counselling and Psychotherapy (www.bac.co.uk)
- Royal College of Psychiatrists (www.rcpsych.ac.uk).

Index